THE OPEN UNIVERSITY
Arts: A Third Level Course
Modern Art and Modernism:
Manet to Pollock

BLOCK VII (Units 15–16)

Abstraction and Kandinsky

Prepared for the Course Team by Sara Selwood

The Open University Press

The Open University Press
Walton Hall
Milton Keynes
MK7 6AA

First published 1983. Reprinted 1988.

Designed by the Graphic Design Group of the Open University.

Text set in 12/13½pt Garamond Medium

Printed in Great Britain by Louis Drapkin Ltd., Birmingham B9 4EA.

ISBN 0 335 11111 4.

This text forms part of an Open University course. The complete list of the course appears at the end of this text.

For general availability of supporting material referred to in this text, please write to Open University Educational Enterprises Limited, 12 Cofferidge Close, Stony Stratford, Milton Keynes, MK11 1BY, Great Britain.

Further information on Open University courses may be obtained from the Admissions Office, The Open University, PO Box 48, Walton Hall, Milton Keynes, MK7 6AB.

1.2

Block VII   Abstraction and Kandinsky

Contents

Set reading

Herschel B. Chipp, *Theories of Modern Art,* University of California Press, 1975.

George Heard Hamilton, *Painting and Sculpture in Europe 1880–1940,* Penguin Books, 1981.

Francis Frascina and Charles Harrison (eds), *Modern Art and Modernism: A Critical Anthology,* Harper and Row, 1982 (referred to as the Reader).

You should read the following texts from the Reader in the course of working through Block VII:

23 Hilla Rebay, 'The Beauty of Non-Objectivity'
25 Wilhelm Worringer, 'Abstraction and Empathy'
26 Hermann Bahr, 'Expressionism'
27 Sheldon Cheney, 'Abstraction and Mysticism'
28 Ernst Gombrich, 'Expression and Communication'

You will also need to read the relevant extracts in the *Supplementary Documents.*

Broadcasting

The following programmes are broadcast while you are working on Block VII.

Television programme 15 *Matisse*
Television programme 16 *Mondrian*
Radiovision programme 15 *A Marxist aesthetic*
Radiovision programme 16 *Marxism and art*

You should look at the notes and illustrations which accompany these programmes before the broadcasts.

The following programmes are also relevant to this block.

Radiovision programme 7 *Symbolism*
Radiovision programme 14 *Der Blaue Reiter*

List of illustrations associated with Block VII

(These are provided in separate booklets. You should refer to the captions printed with the plates for full details of the pictures. Those marked with an asterisk are not referred to in the text but relate to the broadcasts. GMS – Gabriele Münter Stiftung (Gabriele Münter Bequest made in 1957 to the Städtische Galerie im Lenbachhaus, Munich).)

Colour plates

1 Kandinsky, *Picture with White Border*
2 Kandinsky, 'First Abstract Watercolour'
3 Kandinsky, *Improvisation No. 30 (Cannons)*
4 Kandinsky, *The Motley Life*
5 Kandinsky, *Grüngasse in Murnau*
6 Jawlensky, *Yellow Houses*

7 Kandinsky, *Composition 4*
8 Kandinsky, *Small Pleasures*
9 Kandinsky, *All Saints 1*
10 Kandinsky, *Large Resurrection* (woodcut)
*11 Mondrian, *Composition XV in Yellow and Grey*

Black-and-white illustrations

Introduction

Artists first began painting what are usually referred to as 'abstract' pictures in Europe in the second decade of the twentieth century. Those artists who painted 'abstract' pictures did not belong to a movement, nor was there any manifesto of 'abstract art'. As Hamilton points out (page 304) 'abstract art' was practised by a 'number of artists in several different places and at various times'.

Usage of the term 'abstract art' is very problematic. Literally, the verb 'to abstract' means 'to separate or withdraw something from something else'. In this sense, one could argue that all art is abstracted. However, not all 'abstract' works necessarily comprise refined or simplified images taken from a subject. Some artists have made images which they claim resemble nothing. Such images are generally referred to as 'non-figurative', 'non-objective' or 'pure'. Some artists, whose work might be called 'abstract', have insisted on describing their paintings by terms other than 'abstract'. The Alsatian painter Hans (Jean) Arp, for example, referred to his work as 'concrete'.

It could also be argued that all works of art *represent* rather than resemble something. Charles Harrison does precisely this in the *Introduction* (page 24). But if 'abstract' paintings do indeed represent something, how can we decide what it is they are representing?

► Please look at the reproduction of Wassily Kandinsky's *Picture with White Border* (Col.pl.VII.1), a picture which has been generally accepted as being 'abstract'. Can you suggest what it represents? ◄

▷ The first question you probably asked yourself was 'what does it resemble?' When we look at paintings in which there is a high degree of resemblance, for example, Manet's *Bar at the Folies Bergère* (Col.pl.I.17), or even Picasso's *Demoiselles d'Avignon* (Col.pl.V.7) that resemblance establishes guidelines for our understanding of what the painting represents. It is not sufficient for us to be able to understand the work completely, but it does at least provide a starting point. Since 'abstract' paintings, as I have already pointed out, do not appear to bear much resemblance to anything, where should we begin? Perhaps the large white form in Kandinsky's *Picture with White Border* vaguely resembles a wave, and other motifs in the painting suggest a hill. But if our understanding of what the painting represents depended solely on what it resembled, we wouldn't get very far.

In order to find out what this painting might represent we obviously have to ask other questions about it. Towards the end of this introduction I will be discussing what these might be. ◁

Precisely because of the apparently small part played by resemblance in establishing meaning in 'abstract art', the explanation of its origins, and the criticism and interpretation of its subsequent development has often been conducted in terms of formal analysis (see, for example, Hamilton, pages 303–04 which you should read now as it is referred to later). You may well have already found yourself thinking about Kandinsky's painting in terms of his technical or formal concerns, rather than concerning yourself with what it was he was trying to represent. As you will have observed, Alfred H. Barr Jnr. was an influential curator and interpreter of modern art. In the catalogue to the 1936 exhibition, *Cubism and Abstract Art,* held at the Museum of Modern Art, New York, he describes what he calls 'the dialectic of abstract art':

> It is based on the assumption that a work of art, a painting for example, is worth looking at primarily because it presents a composition or organization of colour,

line, light and shade. Resemblance to natural objects, while it does not necessarily destroy these aesthetic values, may easily adulterate their purity. Therefore, since resemblance to nature is at best superfluous and at worst distracting, it might as well be eliminated. . .

Such an attitude of course involves a great impoverishment of painting, an elimination of a wide range of values, such as the connotations of subject matter, sentimental, documentary, political, sexual, religious; the pleasures of easy recognition; and the enjoyment of technical dexterity in the imitation of material forms and surfaces. But in his art the abstract artist prefers impoverishment to adulteration.

(Alfred H. Barr Jnr., *Cubism and Abstract Art*, page 13)

Clearly, Barr considers 'abstract' art antithetical to the kind of art in which a high priority is placed on resemblance. Since he assumes that 'sentimental, documentary, political, sexual' and 'religious' values are eliminated from 'abstract' art, it follows that he is unlikely to assign abstraction any importance in a history of art determined by the 'connotations' of the subject-matter of paintings, or one which examined the historical or social causes of the production of works of art. Instead, he accounts for the evolution of 'abstract' art in terms of purely formal artistic issues. He accordingly claims that 'abstract' art 'developed' because 'the most adventurous and original artists had grown bored with painting facts. By a common and powerful impulse they were driven to abandon the imitation of natural appearances'. Other writers, like Clive Bell, who is discussed in the *Introduction* and in Block XII, subscribed to similar ideas.

According to Barr, against whose view I shall be arguing, this impulse to 'abstraction' was the 'logical and inevitable conclusion towards which art was moving' from Impressionism. Another writer, the American, Donald Gordon, agrees. In an article of 1951 (see References) he wrote: 'Abstraction is the natural climax of the shift away from the exact representation of the Impressionist school. The source of pleasure in the paintings of this school is the organization of colour, line, light, shade and texture'. Furthermore, the two writers identify what they claim to be two 'currents' or 'traditions' of 'abstract' art 'both of which emerged from Impressionism'. According to Gordon, 'The first stems from Cubism and tends to use a technique involving rectilinear, carefully planned geometric forms' (**Pls. VII.1 and 2** and **Col. pl. VIII. 1**). Barr described the second tradition as having 'its principal source in the art and theories of Gauguin and his circle' (**Pls. VII. 3 and 4**), and he thought that this 'flows through the Fauvism of Matisse to the Abstract Expressionism of the pre-war paintings of Kandinsky'. Gordon thought 'paintings of this tradition tend to be vaguely life-like (biomorphic) and curvilinear. The appearance of these later paintings is Romantic and apparently spontaneous'. The diagram overleaf (Figure 1), reproduced from the jacket of Barr's catalogue, shows how he charted the evolution of these two 'traditions'. (It should be noted that the biomorphic 'line' is constructed with Miro/Masson-type Surrealism in mind as the next 'step' on from Kandinsky.)

Barr, and various Modernist critics like him, also proposed that the same 'artistic impulse' was responsible for individual artists' 'development' towards 'abstraction'. Descriptions of Kandinsky's creation of that painting which has become known as the 'First Abstract Watercolour' and was thought to have been painted in 1910. (**Col. pl. VII. 2**) are a case in point. This, for example, is how the critic Dora Vallier (see the 1954 interview with Braque, Block V, page 48) described the advent of 'abstraction' in an article first published in 1975.

It was his lucid acceptance of the elemental power of colour that incited Kandinsky to paint an abstract watercolour. . . One day the spontaneity, the quickness of watercolour took over and the freedom that Kandinsky was looking for was attained. . . pictorial instinct took the upper hand.

(Dora Vallier, 'Colour. His Ariadne's Thread', in *Homage to Wassily Kandinsky*, 1976, page 91.)

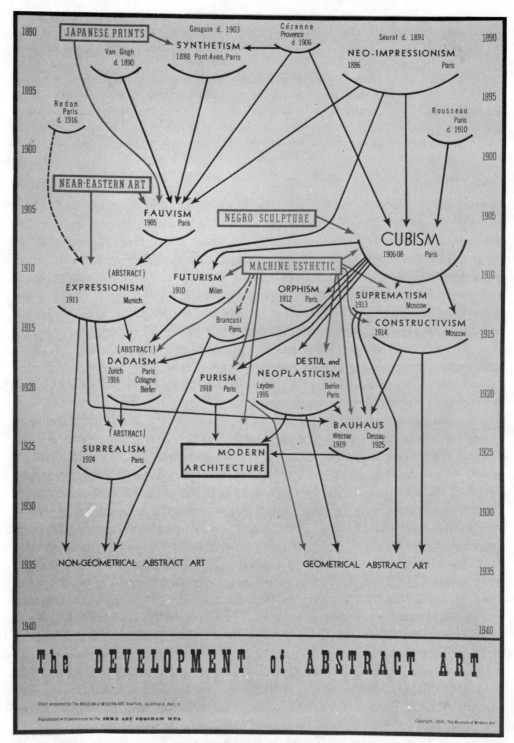

Figure 1 The Development of Abstract Art, 1936. *Chart reproduced from the jacket of Alfred H. Barr Jnr.,* Cubism and Abstract Art, *Museum of Modern Art, New York, 1936. Photograph by courtesy of the Museum of Modern Art, New York.*

The English critic Roger Fry also thought Kandinsky's paintings were the result of 'purely artistic impulses'. The following extract comes from a review he wrote of three of Kandinsky's paintings which were exhibited at the Allied Artists Association in London in 1913. Before reading the extract, please look at the reproduction of *Improvisation No. 30 (Cannons)* (**Col. pl. VII. 3**), one of the paintings Fry was discussing:

> In these {paintings} the forms and colours have no possible justification except the rightness of their relations. That, of course, is really true of all art, but where the representation of natural form comes in, the senses are apt to be tricked into acquiescence by the intelligence. In these improvisations therefore, the form has to

stand the test without any adventitious aids. It seemed to me that they did this and established their rights to be what they were. . . As one contemplates the three one finds that after a time the improvisations become more and more definite, more logical and more closely knit in structure, more surprisingly beautiful their colour oppositions, more exact in their equilibrium. *They are pure visual music.*

(Roger Fry, *The Nation*, 2 August 1913. Quoted after Arthur Jerome Eddy, *Cubists and Post-Impressionism,* pages 116–17)

▶ Please look carefully at **Col. pl. VII. 3** again. What kinds of questions would you want to ask about this painting that Fry did not? ◀

▷ Fry's interpretation of Kandinsky's work is evidently unsatisfactory because it tells us very little that is useful about the kind of pictures being discussed. What it does tell us about is Fry's views on art: his idea that all works of art worthy of the name are characterized by the 'rightness of their relations' or by the analogy to music (both very vague notions). Fry had even used the same stock reference to 'pure visual music' in 1912 to describe the aims of Picasso's Cubist paintings. Fry is not concerned with particular characteristics of Kandinsky's paintings: he makes no reference to *still identifiable objects* in *Improvisation 30;* nor does he refer to its *subject-matter*; he gives us no indication as to *why the picture is painted the way it is;* why it is so *abstracted*; what the artist's *intentions* were; what *ideas* it is based on; for what, or whom it was intended – in short what the causal conditions of the painting were. These are, I hope, the kinds of questions you might have asked. ◁

If we want to find out why particular 'abstract' pictures were painted the way they were, or, more generally, why 'abstraction' evolved at the beginning of this century, we need to employ a different kind of methodology to that of those critics whose writings we have been considering.

One kind of approach we might take was suggested by the American art historian, Meyer Schapiro. In 1937 he published an article entitled 'The Nature of Abstract Art', in the *Marxist Quarterly* (see *Supplementary Documents*, VII.5). It was written in response to Barr's *Cubism and Abstract Art,* of the previous year.

▶ Please read this text very carefully. What does Schapiro object to in Barr's account of 'abstract art'? ◀

▷ Schapiro took Barr to task over numerous points. In particular, he objected to the opposition Barr suggested between 'abstract' and 'representational' art: 'There is', Schapiro wrote, 'no "pure art", unconditioned by experience; all fantasy and formal construction, even the random scribbling of the hand, are shaped by experience and by non-aesthetic concerns'. Because of this he could not accept the notion that any visual object was 'an absolute or pure field or form', or that it could be 'without content'. Nor did he subscribe to Barr's theory of the evolution of 'abstract' art in general. He criticized Barr for presenting it as an 'internal, immanent process among the artists', and for excluding 'as irrelevant to its history the nature of the society in which it arose'. Far from being a 'reaction' to previous styles, as Barr had proposed, Schapiro insisted that 'abstract' art could only have occurred within a specific historical context. He argued that artistic 'reactions' occur 'only under impelling conditions . . . the banal divisions of the great historical styles in . . . art correspond to the momentous divisions in the history of society'. ◁

In this block I will be trying to build on suggestions implicit in Schapiro's article by looking at the historical, intellectual and social circumstances in which early 'abstract' paintings were produced, and, in particular, by considering the diversity of causes which contributed to the advent of 'abstraction'.

In order to do that I will be concentrating on Kandinsky's development towards 'abstract' art up to about 1914, the year he left Munich to return to Russia. Of all the early 'abstract' painters, Kandinsky is one of the most interesting to study, not least because he has been constantly singled out by historians of modern art as 'the first abstract painter', a title to which he himself laid claim in his later years (see pages 45 ff). As you will have seen from Hamilton's account of 'abstract' painting (pages 303–4) Kandinsky could never be described as a typical 'abstract' painter. No 'abstract' painter could. However, he was committed to an *idea* of 'abstract' art, writing about it, and practising it from about 1913 until his death in 1944.

Besides producing a large number of paintings, Kandinsky was also a very prolific and influential writer; between 1909 and 1944 he wrote two books and more than seventy articles on art. His writings tell us a great deal about his development towards 'abstraction' (even if they do not explain it). In addition, they provide us with a record of the ideas which contributed to his theories and practice. I believe they also influenced subsequent writings about and interpretations of modern art, and of 'abstract' art in particular.

Kandinsky raises several specific problems and issues relevant to a consideration of modern art as a whole. His theories, particularly, are entrenched within what we have come to recognize as a Modernist critical tradition. Many issues aired in his writings are particularly pertinent to this course. For instance, according to his account, a very high priority is placed on the 'expressive', as opposed to the 'representational' function of his paintings, a characteristic of modern art frequently referred to throughout the theoretical, critical and interpretative literature on the subject.

Kandinsky's writings are interesting in the context of this course for another reason. His paintings have often been interpreted in terms of what *he said he was trying to do*: that is, many critical interpretations of his works have been based on his own writings. One way of reassessing his position in the histories of modern art would be to consider the value of referring to those writings. Do they provide us with a sufficient account of his works, or do we need to look elsewhere for more information about contemporary ideas which might have 'shaped his experience'? We might also test the validity of many assumptions upon which Modernist accounts of his work are based: was Kandinsky a painter of 'abstract' pictures? To what degree are the paintings he produced up to *c.* 1914 'abstract'? Are his views, or even his paintings, representative of a general trend towards 'abstract' art at the beginning of this century, or do they only seem to be so in retrospect?

In order to try and answer or, at least, point the way to answering these questions, Kandinsky will be considered in this block in the following way.

In *Part 1*, I will be looking at Kandinsky's social and cultural background; contemporary art in Russia and Germany; his training; his intellectual milieu and the ideas associated with it, and the nature of his own theoretical interests.

In *Part 2*, I will be looking at the development of Kandinsky's painting, in particular following the publication of his major theoretical treatise, *On the Spiritual in Art*, 1911. I will be considering the relationship between Kandinsky's art and his theory, and suggesting what kinds of causes might account for the appearance of Kandinsky's painting.

In *Part 3*, I will be considering late nineteenth- and early twentieth-century notions of 'abstract' art in order to see how these might have influenced Kandinsky's ideas, and those of his contemporaries. I will also be comparing different critical interpretations of Kandinsky's work, and considering how Kandinsky's own retrospective account of his development towards 'abstraction' may have affected those critical views. Finally, I will be considering some of the difficulties raised by interpretations of 'abstract' art.

1 Kandinsky's artistic and ideological background

Kandinsky's Russian background

Wassily Kandinsky was born into a middle-class family in Moscow in 1866: his father worked as a manager in a tea firm. As a child, Kandinsky liked drawing and had private drawing lessons. However, art was not his original choice of career: in 1886 he registered at Moscow University to study law, economics and politics and his subsequent academic career was evidently successful. In 1889 he went with an expedition to the province of Vologda to report on usages of peasant law for the faculty of Natural Science, Anthropology and Ethnography of the University of Moscow, and later published his findings in two articles in ethnographic journals. In about 1893 he was appointed to a position in the Law Faculty at the University. This was probably a *Privatdozent*, a non-salaried teaching post, usually held by scholars of private means (see pages 20 ff for a discussion of Kandinsky's income). He later declined the offer of a lectureship at the University of Dorpat. In about 1895 he gave up his academic career and worked as a manager in one of the largest printing firms in Moscow. After a year, at the age of thirty, he left Russia to study art in Munich.

According to his autobiographical essay 'Reminiscences', published in Munich in 1913 (see Appendix A, page 55) virtually the only art Kandinsky knew before leaving Russia was 'realistic art, in fact only the Russians'. The art he was referring to was that produced by members of the large group, 'The Wanderers' or 'The Society of Wandering (or Travelling) Exhibitions', founded in 1871. As their name suggests, the Wanderers' paintings were shown throughout Russia. During the 1870s and 1880s they exhibited in all the major provincial capitals, including Odessa to which Kandinsky's family had moved in about 1871. The Wanderers had no official affiliations, but were sponsored by private collectors of Russian art, including Pavel Tretyakov, whose collection later formed the basis of the Tretyakov Museum of Russian Art (see Block VIII). Most of the artists who founded the Wanderers had resigned from the St Petersburg Academy of Art in 1863 principally because they objected to the subject set for the Academy's Gold Award for history painting. That year it was the 'Banquet of the Gods at Valhalla'. Like the French 'Realists' discussed in Block I they objected to the kinds of mythological, classical and romantic themes favoured by the Academy. They thought art should be concerned with representing aspects of contemporary life in Russia. Many of their paintings depict landscape and genre subjects. Some, though by no means most, show scenes with obvious political or social connotations, for example, the corruption of the Church. Kandinsky remembered that as a boy he had been particularly impressed by one of the Wanderers' paintings – Repin's *They Did Not Expect Him* (Pl.VII.5), which depicts the unexpected return home of a political prisoner. (Unfortunately he never explained why it had appealed to him.)

Kandinsky also admired Russian folk art which he first encountered in 'its true and original setting' in Vologda, a very remote province (see Figure 2 overleaf). In

Figure 2 Map showing the location of
Vologda, from W. H. Parker, An Historical
Geography of Russia, *University of London*
Press, 1968. Copyright: Hodder and
Stoughton, Sevenoaks.

'Reminiscences' he remembered how on entering peasants' houses there, he saw that all the objects were

> . . . covered with brightly coloured, elaborate ornaments. Folk pictures on the walls: a symbolic representation of a hero, a battle, a painted folk song . . . When I finally entered the room, I felt surrounded on all sides by painting, into which I had thus penetrated.

('Reminiscences', 1913, *Kandinsky. Complete Writings on Art*, 1982, page 369).

Kandinsky suggested these experiences shaped his conceptions about painting: 'For many years I have sought the possibility of letting the viewer "stroll" within the picture, forcing him to become absorbed in the picture, forgetful of himself'.

Kandinsky's appreciation of those peasant handicrafts should be seen in relation to the general contemporary interest in peasant and primitive culture. From the end of the nineteenth century, members of the Russian intelligentsia, like their French and German counterparts (see Block III, page 32, and Block IV, page 37) became fascinated by indigenous peasant cultures. One effect of the Industrial Revolution in Russia, which, as in Germany, occurred later than in Britain, was that peasants were changing their old beliefs and practices along with their traditional way of life. In the same way that ethnographers like Kandinsky studied the peasant criminal law of what he described as 'the fishing and hunting communities of the slowly disappearing Syrenians, to salvage the remnants of their pagan religion? ('Reminiscences', 1913, *Kandinsky. Complete Writings*, page 365) so collectors and scholars became interested in *Lubki* (primitive hand-coloured broadsides **Pls. VII.6 and 7**), icons, embroidery and peasant pottery. Rovinskii, for example, edited and published a five-volume collection of *Lubki* from 1881 onwards, and the critic Stasov published a comprehensive work on popular Russian ornament, *Slav and Eastern Ornament.*

There were also practical attempts to preserve the handicrafts. Collectors like Savva Ivanovich Mamontov (1841–1918) and Princess Maria Tenisheva (1867–1928), who both owned large private country estates, commissioned peasant-style architecture (Figure 3) and established craft workshops. Large numbers of local

Figure 3 Abramtsevo Church, 1880–82, an example of the Russian neo-nationalist style. Society for Cultural Relations with the USSR, London.

peasants were employed to work in these. The embroidery workshop at Princess Tenisheva's estate, Talashkino, for instance, involved 2,000 peasant women and 50 villages. Products from these workshops were sold commercially. However, the kinds of goods produced were by no means authentic. As the historian of Russian art, John Bowlt, has observed, the workshops tended to follow the highly eclectic fashion of the 1870s, indiscriminately transferring folk motifs and patterns from one medium to another; a process which inspired one critic to compare contemporary Neo-nationalist Russian architecture to 'marble hand-woven towels and brick embroideries' (Figure 4). In the 1870s attempts were also made to protect small

Figure 4 Tretyakov Gallery, 1872–74, in the neo-nationalist style. Photo from V. Marcadé, Le Renouveau de l'art pictural russe 1863–1914, *Editions L'Age d'Homme, 1971.*

craftsmen from commercial exploitation by the provision of economic and social benefits.

Kandinsky remained interested in folk art after he went to live in Bavaria. As you will have noticed, a concern with primitive art is characteristic of modern art (see *Introduction* page 50 and Block IV, pages 47ff). As we shall see later in this block, many of Kandinsky's ideas about 'abstract' art and 'expressivity' can be related to notions of primitivism.

Until about the 1890s Russians were generally unaware of contemporary European art. Because of this, Kandinsky, who was used to the work of the Wanderers, was extremely surprised when he first encountered Impressionism. This would probably have been in 1896 when a large touring exhibition of French art, including a section of works by contemporary painters, was shown in Moscow. One of the paintings he saw was a Monet 'Haystack in Sunlight', like Pl. VII.8. Unfortunately we cannot be sure exactly which particular painting it was, since the catalogue gives no detail of the works in the exhibition. Kandinsky described his reaction to seeing the painting in 'Reminiscences':

> . . . Suddenly, for the first time, I saw a *picture*. That it was a haystack, the catalogue informed me. I didn't recognize it. I found this non-recognition painful, and thought that the painter had no right to paint so indistinctly. I had a dull feeling that the object was lacking in this picture. And I noticed with some surprise and confusion that the picture not only gripped me, but impressed itself ineradicably upon my memory, always hovering quite unexpectedly before my eyes, down to the last detail. It was all unclear to me, and I was not able to draw the simple conclusions from this experience. What was, however, clear to me was the unsuspected power of the palette, previously concealed from me, which exceeded all my dreams. Painting took on a fairy-tale power and splendour. And, albeit unconsciously, objects were discredited as an essential element within the picture.
>
> (Kandinsky, 'Reminiscences', *Kandinsky. Complete Writings on Art*, page 363)

► Please read Kandinsky's description from 'Reminiscences' over again and look carefully at the reproduction of the Monet, *Haystacks, End of Summer* (Pl. VII.8) as well as that of another picture which had impressed him, Repin's *They Did Not Expect Him* (Pl. VII.5).

The two paintings are clearly very different. What kinds of interests are they likely to have held for Kandinsky? ◄

▷ In very crude (Modernist) terms it could be said that Monet's painting displays the artist's considerable interest in the medium of paint and the way it can be applied to the surface of the canvas, and that the subject matter held relatively little interest for him. By comparison, a Modernist might say of the Repin that the means are not emphasized and that although they obviously contribute to the overall content of the painting, the narrative is of primary importance. ◁

This comparison shows us how plausible it might seem for Modernists to oppose characteristics of resemblance and formal functions in works of art. It was precisely this 'opposition' that was at the forefront of Kandinsky's mind when he wrote that passage in 'Reminiscences'. Even in 1896 when he first saw Monet's 'Haystack in Sunlight', Kandinsky was doubtless aware of these issues. By 1901, the year he published his first article on art, 'Critique of Critics', he was certainly party to critical debates concerning them. In this article he set out to censure the critical viewpoint that was prevalent in Russia at that time – the view that the artist should devote 'his life to acquiring the capacity of recording anything that enters his field of vision', and that the value of a work of art lay in its accessibility. In his famous

1897 treatise, *What is Art?* the Russian writer Tolstoi had claimed that 'great works of art are only great because they are accessible and comprehensible to everyone'. Critics who thought this, and the 'Realist' painters they supported, were disdainful of contemporary French painting. Repin, for example, who had even studied in Paris from about 1873–74, disliked, or at least chose not to sympathize with French art. In a letter to the critic Stasov, whom Kandinsky also attacked, he wrote: 'Modern French painting is so empty, so ridiculous in content; the painting is talented but there's only painting . . . no content at all'. As we shall see later many implications raised by this debate had a formative influence on Kandinsky's later theories and his conception of 'abstraction'.

Kandinsky in Munich

Figure 5 Kandinsky posing with sword, c. 1901. Städtische Galerie im Lenbachhaus, München.

Munich had many attractions as a place to study art. From the middle of the nineteenth century it had been regarded as a major centre for academic study, second only to Paris. It was quite common for educated and wealthy Russians to study abroad. Kandinsky probably chose to study in Munich rather than Paris because he could speak German. As a child it had been his second language.

By the end of the nineteenth century Munich had become one of the major German art centres. You may find it useful to reread Gill Perry's section on Germany at the turn of the century (Block IV, pages 35–8) before continuing. Contemporary commentators often remarked on the sheer amount of artistic activity in the city of Munich. In his book *Munich: History, Monuments, Art*, published in 1910, Henry Rawle Wadleigh, for example, observed:

> It is a notable fact that in a commercial age, one great city should be conscious of herself as a centre of art rather than a centre of industry . . . Munich, a city of 600,000 inhabitants has few factories; works of art and beer are the only products that Munich exports in any considerable quantity. A very large proportion of her

people are economically non-productive. Students, artists, foreign residents (it is difficult for a non-Bavarian to obtain work in Munich) and members of the leisure class who live upon their incomes . . . the number of musicians, painters and other artists is said to exceed 10,000 . . .

(Henry Rawle Wadleigh, *Munich: History, Monuments, Art,* pp. 11, 91–92)

What kinds of artistic activities went on in Munich? Art there was traditionally patronized by the Wittelsbach family, the Bavarian Monarchy. Their collections formed the basis of later museum and public collections in the city, making Munich the centre of art in Bavaria. They also contributed to the city's international reputation and its role as the most important art market in Central Europe in the second half of the century. Munich almost certainly acquired this position because it was the first city in Germany to possess two large permanent exhibition halls: the *Kunstausstellungsgebäude* and the *Glaspalast*, both of which were founded by the monarchy. The *Glaspalast*, as you can see from Figure 6, was a vast iron and glass structure. It was based on the Crystal Palace in London (1851), and was the first building of its kind to be erected on the Continent. In 1869 it was used for the first international art exhibition which contained over 4,500 works. This exhibition was responsible for introducing a large amount of contemporary French painting to Munich. Throughout the 1870s and 1880s the Munich Artists' Association (*Künstlergenossenschaft*) held their annual exhibitions at the *Glaspalast*, each exhibition comprising thousands of canvases.

Figure 6 Poppel and Kurz, The Glass Palace (Der Glaspalast), *1854. Photograph of an engraving, Münchner Stadtmuseum, München.*

In 1892, 78 artists, including Franz Stuck, Kandinsky's second teacher, resigned from the Munich Artists' Association to form the Munich *Secession* (splinter group). The Secessionists intended showing work representative of various tendencies in contemporary art. They were neither reacting against academic art as such, nor championing any particular direction of style. By 1896 the *Secession* already appeared to be on the wane, and returned to exhibit with the Munich Artists' Association. Their reasons for doing so were possibly financial.

As already mentioned the *Glaspalast* was of vital importance to the economic success of the Munich art market. A contemporary commentator reported that the Munich international art exhibition of 1888 (by then an annual show) registered sales of 1,070,000 Marks, half the total being spent on works by German artists. In 1901 the President of the Munich Artists' Association boasted of a steady increase in the annual income from sales at the annual *Glaspalast* exhibition. That year it stood at 770,000 Marks, about £1,000,000 in present day terms. In his theoretical writings and reviews Kandinsky was to criticize severely the commercial motivation of those artists who participated in exhibitions such as those held at the *Glaspalast*.

Kandinsky's training and his activities within the Munich art world

Kandinsky's first teacher was the Yugoslav painter, Anton Ažbè (1840–1905) whose school (Figure 7) was located in Munich's bohemian quarter, Schwabing. Kandinsky registered at Ažbè's in 1896. According to various contemporary sources, it was the 'biggest' and 'most famous' private school in the city, and attracted students of the highest social standing as well as large numbers of Russian students. One of Ažbè's first students was the Russian painter, Bilibin (see page 24). It was here that Kandinsky met two compatriots who were to become close friends and be associated with the *Neue Künstler Vereinigung* and the *Blaue Reiter* exhibitions that he helped to organize (pages 22ff). They were Alexej Jawlensky (1864–1941), and his mistress, Marianne Werefkin. Kandinsky left Ažbè's in 1897. According to one of his contemporaries, the Russian 'socialist realist', Igor Grabar, Kandinsky 'was not very successful at Ažbè's school and didn't seem

Figure 7 The studio of Anton Ažbè, c. 1896. Narodna Galerija, Ljubljana.

talented'. He may have already found himself unsympathetic to the kind of work Ažbè produced. His *In the Harem*, c. 1905 (**Pl. VII.9**) was precisely the kind of painting Kandinsky critically attacked in later years (see page 31). According to Grabar, while still one of Ažbè's students he had already yielded to the influence of *World of Art* stylization (see pages 24ff). By his own account Kandinsky was not a diligent student: he often cut classes and went to paint in Schwabing, or 'stayed at home and tried to paint a picture from memory . . . or imagination'. He claimed that he found working from models degrading. It was all the more surprising, therefore, that on leaving Ažbè's he was determined to be admitted into Franz Stuck's atelier. Stuck, as Kandinsky observed, was reputed to be 'Germany's best draughtsman'.

According to the German painter Hans Purrman, 'to be admitted into Stuck's class was proof and recognition of a talent of which one could be proud'. Stuck was renowned as the most 'successful' artist in Munich; he frequently won gold medals at the *Glaspalast* exhibitions, and had been the youngest painter to be made a professor at the Academy. He was known as 'the Prince' of art in Munich, and he lived in the kind of style he thought most compatible with his professional stature. Having married a wealthy American widow Stuck designed and built for himself an imposing palatial villa on the banks of the Isar River, the Villa Stuck (Figure 8).

Figure 8   Villa Stuck with poplars. Stuck-Jugendstil-Verein E.V.

Kandinsky only remained in Stuck's class for a year. In later years he was disparaging about his former teacher. In 1910, in one of his 'Letters from Munich', he commented on how Stuck's works appeared with monotonous regularity in exhibitions of the 'soulless Munich school': 'Year after year . . . the cheerless call of the fat trumpet: Stuck, Stuck, Stuck! . . . This kind of art, or what passes for art, is like a well-made, brightly painted, dead, utterly dead doll – see what the Munich exhibitions have substituted for the live, striking, vibrant, stirring spirit'. However, it is possible that Stuck exerted some influence on Kandinsky's work. In

'Reminiscences' he described how Stuck objected to his 'excesses of colour', making him work in black and white, something which may have led to his later facility with graphics. Types of images Stuck favoured – guardian angels of peace, the serpent of evil, the mystical horseman recur in Kandinsky's works transformed into 'abstract' symbols (see pages 36ff). Kandinsky sometimes emulated Stuck's formal style. Compare, for example, the poster Stuck designed for the *Secession* with one Kandinsky designed for the *Phalanx* a few years later (**Pls. VII.11, 12**). Kandinsky may also have been influenced by Stuck's interest in craft work. His paintings were sometimes presented in highly elaborated frames, as if they were objects of applied art (see **Pl. VIII.10**), and he was renowned for his designs for silverware, furniture, etc. Through his association with the applied arts, Stuck's name became inexorably linked with *Jugendstil*, the decorative art movement which flourished in Munich in the 1890s. According to several art historians, Peg Weiss particularly, *Jugendstil* was also one of Kandinsky's most important formative influences.

Jugendstil (literally, youth style) is the German version of the French and Belgian *art nouveau*. It derived its name from the journal *Die Jugend*, founded in Munich in 1896. According to the social historian, Peter Jelavich, its aims were to rejuvenate the liberal middle classes politically and aesthetically and to encourage them to overcome their subservience to the Catholic Church's morals and attitudes which prevailed in Munich at the time. (The Catholic Centre Party had held control in the Bavarian Parliament from 1869, and continued to do so until the end of the First World War.) A similar ideological standpoint was promoted by *Simplicissimus*, a satirical magazine founded at the same time.

In the 1982 exhibition catalogue *Kandinsky in Munich*, Peter Jelavich suggested that the characteristics of *Jugendstil*, 'strong linear outlines, flat planes of bright colour and a wilful stylization of . . . objects to achieve either ornamental or comic effects . . .' (see **Pl. VII.13**) proved perfectly suited to the goals of *Die Jugend*. He also maintains that *Jugendstil* was a 'socially ambiguous phenomenon'. Although it originated as a supposedly culturally rejuvenating, sensuous and satirical movement, some of its practitioners attempted to transform it into a personal and spiritual medium. They were only a minority, but their ideas are worth discussing here, because, as we shall see later, they may well have influenced Kandinsky's theories about the language of 'abstract' art.

Before 1900, the artists, Adolf Hölzel, Hermann Obrist and August Endell were becoming convinced that the linear elements of *Jugendstil* (previously conceived of as ornamental) could be used to evoke powerful sensations. Between 1896 and 1898 Endell wrote about the possibility of a new kind of art comprising 'forms that signify nothing, represent nothing, but that will be able to excite our souls as deeply as only music has been able to do with tones'. He conceived of an artistic language, which would not be based on motifs resembling objects, but which might evoke associations arousing certain emotions in an observer. He thought different types of line could stimulate different kinds of psychological effects in the same way natural objects might. (Similar ideas had influenced Seurat's work ten years earlier.) According to Endell, the appreciation of such an art would be restricted to the visually 'sensitive':

> He who has never been delighted by the exquisite bendings of the blade of grass, by the wonderful inexorability of the thistle, the austere youthfulness of the sprouting leaf buds . . . and stirred to the depths of his soul, . . . knows nothing about the beauty of forms.
>
> (August Endell, *Um die Schönheit* (*On Beauty*), page 11. Quoted in Peg Weiss, *Kandinsky in Munich*, 1979, page 38)

As you will remember from the *Introduction* (page 44), the notion that art can only be appreciated by an elite is characteristic of much Modernist theorizing. It was a notion which also attracted Kandinsky.

By the time Kandinsky left Stuck's atelier he was thirty-four. He still continued to receive a private income from his father. Apparently no details about his income are known, but we can estimate what this might have been from some of his outgoings. We know, for instance, that between 1901 and 1908 Kandinsky spent a considerable amount of money on travelling. He travelled extensively both abroad and in Germany, often in the company of his mistress Gabriele Münter (Figure 9). He visited Italy (Venice and the Riviera), Tunis, Holland, France (Paris and Sèvres where he lived for a year in 1907) and Switzerland. In addition, Kandinsky visited Russia nearly every year up until 1914.

Figure 9 Gabriele Münter in Dresden, 1905 (photograph by Kandinsky). Städtische Galerie im Lenbachhaus, München.

We also know something about the costs of his living accommodation. In 1909 Münter, who also came from a wealthy family, bought a house in the Bavarian countryside near Murnau. The previous year Kandinsky had started renting a spacious flat in Schwabing (Figure 10). According to his biographer, Will Grohmann, his rent was 1,400 Marks a year, a considerable amount. We also know that housekeepers were employed in both homes. In addition to these outgoings, Kandinsky at least partly financed the exhibitions and school associated with a society to which he belonged, the *Phalanx*.

Taking all these details into consideration, one can probably estimate that Kandinsky's income would have amounted to well over 3,000 Marks a year, placing him within the wealthiest six per cent of the German population. According to figures presented in Hajo Holborn's book, *A History of Modern Germany 1840–1945*, in 1900 the national average income was only 603 Marks a year. In Prussia, where incomes were lower than the national average, 62 per cent of the population earned less than 900 Marks a year. In Bavaria, where Kandinsky lived, incomes were even lower than those in Prussia. Judging by these figures, Kandinsky's rent alone came to more than twice the average national earnings.

What kinds of implications can we draw from these facts? Obviously, Kandinsky's income freed him from the practical necessity and constraints of having to earn a living. He had no need to produce paintings of commercial value, such as those

Figure 10 Kandinsky's mother in his flat, 36, Ainmillerstrasse, Munich, 1913 (photograph by Kandinsky). Städtische Galerie im Lenbachhaus, München.

shown every year at the Munich Artists' Association's exhibitions. He was free to indulge his own interests and aspirations. This position conceivably influenced some of his views, for example, his image of the artist as an isolated, yet messianic individual at odds with society producing a kind of art incomprehensible to the majority of mankind, yet at the same time vital for its 'spiritual' future.

When Kandinsky left Stuck's atelier in late 1900 aged thirty-four, he began to make his mark on the Munich art world, surprisingly for an inexperienced newcomer just out of art school. He organized exhibitions for the *Phalanx*; taught painting in his own school; became involved in the arts and crafts movement; published articles and reviews, and submitted works to exhibitions throughout Europe and Russia.

Little is known about the origins or demise of the *Phalanx*. The society had its own exhibition rooms near the *Secession*, where it mounted shows by young artists as well as 'invited guests'. The eleven exhibitions Kandinsky organized were very diverse. He showed works by contemporaries in Stuck's atelier; representatives of various local artists' communities; members of the Munich *Secession*; practitioners of the applied arts. Among the 'invited guests' who exhibited were Monet, Lautrec, and the 'Neo-Impressionists', Signac, and Theo van Rysselberghe. We also know that Kandinsky intended exhibiting the work of Pissarro. This kind of eclecticism characterized all Kandinsky's activities during this period.

These exhibitions were important in introducing contemporary foreign art to Munich. It was only later that other Munich galleries and dealers followed suit. In 1906 the *Kunstverein* exhibited works from Schuffenecker's collection, including paintings by Cézanne, Van Gogh, Gauguin and Matisse (see Block III A); in 1908, Brakl (whose gallery Kandinsky described as 'the most advanced gallery in Munich') showed a large Van Gogh exhibition; in 1909, Cézannes were shown at the *Secession*, and in 1910 the Moderne Galerie Thannhauser had Manet and Gauguin exhibitions.

Kandinsky subsequently became involved with the *Neue Künstler-Vereinigung München* (the New Artists' Society of Munich), which aimed to mount exhibitions in Germany and abroad, organizing lectures, publications and other related events. In particular, it promoted a subjective approach to the creation of works of art. The majority of the society's members were painters, many were friends of Kandinsky and Münter, including Jawlensky and Werefkin. However, the membership also included writers, theoreticians and artists working in different fields, for example the Russian dancer, Aleksandr Sakharov. The NKVM's first and second exhibitions were held in the prestigious Thannhauser gallery, after the newly appointed director of the Bavarian State Collections, Hugo von Tschudi interceded with Thannhauser on behalf of these largely unknown artists. You will find details of the second exhibition in Hamilton, page 207.

Kandinsky's activities were not just concerned with exhibitions. From 1901 he began publishing articles and reviews, and in 1911 he started work with the Bavarian painter, Franz Marc, on plans for an annual publication called the *Blaue Reiter* (*The Blue Rider Almanac*). Kandinsky intended 'to compile a book . . . in which the articles would be exclusively by artists', and which would emphasize what Kandinsky called a 'synthesis', a close-knit relationship, between modern painting and other kinds of art, usually considered to be unrelated. These included art of ethnographical interest, children's art and folk art. Kandinsky also wanted to show that apparently disparate tendencies within modern art – 'abstraction' and 'representation' for example – were related (see his *Blaue Reiter* essay, 'On the Problem of Form', translated in Chipp, page 155 ff). In the end, one edition of the *Blaue Reiter* was published in 1912 by the Munich publisher Reinhard Piper, who later published Kandinsky's books, *On the Spiritual in Art* and *Klänge* (*Sounds*). Financial support for the project was given by the Berlin industrialist, Bernard Köhler, whose niece was married to Marc's friend, the painter August Macke, editor of all the ethnographical material for the almanac. (The *Blaue Reiter* is discussed more fully in Radiovision programme 14.)

Figure 11 Kandinsky and his friends from the Blaue Reiter *period; Kandinsky seated; from left to right, Maria Marc, Franz Marc, Bernhard Köhler, Heinrich Campendonck, Thomas von Hartmann (photograph by Gabriele Münter). Städtische Galerie im Lenbachhaus, München.*

Marc and Kandinsky resigned from the NKVM in 1911, and the two artists rapidly began assembling a collection of paintings in what Kandinsky called 'a purely dictatorial manner', these were to be exhibited as an alternative to the NKVM's third exhibition (see Hamilton, page 213). The aims of the exhibition, which went under the title 'The First Exhibition of the Editors of the *Blaue Reiter*' (Figure 12), recalled those of the almanac – to show works which did not conform to 'any one precise tendency, but rather the multiplicity of way in which the spirit is made manifest'. Among those artists represented were the Germans, August Macke and Heinrich Campendonck, the Russian Burliuk brothers, Robert Delaunay, Henri Rousseau and the composer, Arnold Schoenberg, as well as Kandinsky, Marc and Münter.

Figure 12 Photograph by Gabriele Münter of first Blaue Reiter *Exhibition, 1911–1912. Gabriele Münter- und Johannes Eichner-Stiftung, München.*

'The Second Exhibition of the Editors of the *Blaue Reiter*', held in the Hans Goltz gallery in Munich, was far more ambitious than the first. It was conceived as a review of contemporary European tendencies in the graphic arts, and included work by Marc, Paul Klee, Alfred Kubin, Picasso, Heckel and Natalia Goncharova.

Kandinsky's refusal to identify himself with any particular tendency within contemporary art typified his other artistic activities, for example, exhibiting his own work. According to Donald Gordon's list of 'Modern Art Exhibitions' Kandinsky participated in 83 exhibitions between 1902 and 1914. This list is not totally inclusive – Kandinsky probably exhibited *more* often. This is remarkable considering that Kandinsky did not depend on sales of works to support himself. Why did he exhibit so often? Can we deduce anything from the variety of exhibitions he participated in? Kandinsky had no affiliation with any gallery or dealer which prevented him from showing elsewhere, unlike the Kahnweiler contracts (see Block V). Even in 1913 when he became closely associated with Herwarth Walden of *Der Stürm* in Berlin, he continued to exhibit works as before.

Kandinsky apparently attached no significance to the contexts within which his works were shown. He exhibited with groups of whose policies or standards he disapproved. For example, in 1902, he exhibited with the Munich *Secession*. Despite writing disparaging reviews of the *Secession's* exhibitions he nevertheless applied to show with them on three subsequent occasions. Evidently, Kandinsky wanted his work to be seen as much, and in as many places, as possible. He refused to identify himself with any particular exhibiting group because he claimed to be opposed to any categorization of art (see his *Blaue Reiter* essay, 'On the Problem of Form', in Chipp, page 158), although this is what he sometimes seems to be doing in his own publications.

What of Kandinsky's work during his years in Munich? Was that also eclectic? Before 1914 Kandinsky was open to various technical influences. He became in-volved with the *Jugendstil* movement in Munich after leaving Stuck's studio and the first exhibition he organized for the *Phalanx* in 1902 was almost entirely devoted to *Jugendstil* and craft works; in 1904 he became actively involved with the *Vereinigung für angewandte Kunst* (the Society for Applied Art), and between 1902 and 1906 he showed designs and craftworks at various exhibitions, including the Salon d'Automne of 1905 and 1906 in Paris. These included woodcuts, which were then classified as 'applied', rather than 'fine' art. Kandinsky also designed jewellery, furniture, locks and keys, embroidery and ceramics (see **Pls.VII.14–16**). One might be tempted to try to distinguish between Kandinsky's work as a designer and as a painter, but his activities as a designer probably influenced and had implica-tions for his painting.

Kandinsky's links with the Russian art world

While Kandinsky lived in Munich he retained close links with Russia and the Russian art world. He had several Russian friends, exhibited his work regularly in Russian exhibitions, and published numerous articles in Russian magazines and journals. He also merited some attention in Russia himself. Beween 1904 and 1914 at least fifty-one articles mentioning Kandinsky appeared in the Russian press.

As we have already seen (pages 11 ff) during the 1870s and the 1880s many Russian critics believed art should be used to record contemporary reality. This attitude characterized the work of the Realists. But there was an alternative view-point. In 1898 a new and sumptuously produced journal, *Mir Iskusstva* (*World of Art*, **Pl.VII.18**) was founded by the theatre and ballet producer Sergei Diaghilev and it remained in publication until 1904. It was initially sponsored by the collec-tors Mamontov and Princess Tenisheva, and later by Tzar Nicholas II. Although it is hard to associate the *World of Art* with any particular stance, in general it prop-osed a Symbolist viewpoint which was seen by many of its sympathizers, including Kandinsky, as being diametrically opposed to that of the Realists. I will shortly be discussing the Realist/Symbolist debate and its implications for Kandinsky. Mean-while I want to look briefly at the kinds of interests which characterized the *World of Art* artists' work.

Two particular characteristics of their work are worth considering in relation to Kandinsky's painting. Some *World of Art* artists like Alexander Benois and Leon Bakst made highly intricate designs for vignettes and other ornamental works. Historical themes were also typical. Benois and Konstantin Somov, for example, depicted scenes of the epoch of the Sun King at Versailles (**Pl.VII.17**), which in contrast with contemporary Russian life seemed to them to embody a certain kind of elegance and escapism. Other artists, like Ivan Bilibin preferred to represent medieval scenes (**Pl.VII.19**), usually as illustrations for new editions of Russian fairy tales. These should be considered in the context of the contemporary interest in indigenous Russian culture (see pages 11 ff).

▶ Please look at Kandinsky's painting of 1907 *The Motley Life* (Col.pl.VII.4). What might have influenced the artist's choice of subject-matter and technique? What kinds of interests are represented in this picture? In order to answer these questions you may find it useful to look back over some of the points already raised in this block. ◀

▷ Judging from the architectural details of the fortified castle and the priest's garb, *The Motley Life* appears to represent a Russian scene. Kandinsky has shown various activities taking place: rowing, lovers embracing, men engaged in battle, and so on. The painting also includes very diverse figures: a knight on horseback, a Russian monk with a cowl decorated with a skull and cross bones, a beggar, etc. As we shall see, many of these images were to assume an iconographic significance in Kandinsky's later paintings in which they appear either combined or individually. The kinds of images represented in *The Motley Life* bear little resemblance to aspects of contemporary reality. The picture looks as if it were painted from the artist's imagination. In his 'Cologne Lecture' of 1914 Kandinsky actually described how in *The Motley Life* he had 'created many things from within myself'. In what he called his 'Russian Period' he claimed to have drawn 'everything from memory and according to my mental picture'. As I suggested in the introduction (page 6), even the most apparently subjective works are influenced by experience of some kind, and we should perhaps treat Kandinsky's assertions with a degree of scepticism. It seems to me that *The Motley Life* belongs to the same contemporary convention as the work of the *World of Art* artists, like Bilibin and Somov.

What about the way the picture is painted? *The Motley Life* is very brightly coloured and the paint is applied in flat patches over what appears to be a dark ground. Kandinsky's technique of mixing small dots and patches of colour recalls that of the Neo-Impressionists, with whose work he was familiar (see page 21). This is even more apparent in another painting by Kandinsky – his *Beach Chairs in Holland* of 1904 (Pl.VII.20). While the Neo-Impressionists used the pointillist technique to render natural light effects more systematically, in Kandinsky's hands it becomes an essentially decorative device. In fact, he used this technique in earlier decorative designs (see Pl.VII.14). The way that some areas of *Motley Life* are painted, are reminiscent of the beadwork on those items Münter executed after Kandinsky's designs (Pl.VII.16). Furthermore, according to the 'Cologne Lecture', Kandinsky had intended producing an essentially decorative, formalized painting:

> In *Colourful Life* [*The Motley Life*] . . . the task that charmed me most was that of creating a confusion of masses, patches, lines. I used a 'bird's eye view' to place the figures one above the other. To arrange the dividing-up of areas and the application of the brushstrokes as I wished, on each occasion I had to find a perspective pretext or excuse.
>
> (Kandinsky, 'Cologne Lecture', *Kandinsky. Complete Writings on Art*, page 395) ◁

Kandinsky's painting was open to other influences. When he and Münter returned to Munich after nearly a year of travelling (page 20), Kandinsky began painting at Murnau, often in the company of Jawlensky, who had attended Matisse's classes in Paris. Kandinsky's paintings of the period are characteristically very bright (see Col.pl.VII.5), and are often referred to as 'Fauvist'. Surprisingly, Kandinsky had not painted like this when he and Münter lived near Paris (1906–7). He seems to have needed Jawlensky's example to stimulate him to paint in this way. If we compare the two artists' Murnau pictures we find striking similarities (cf. Col.pls.VII.5 and VII.6, and Pls.VII.4 and VII.21). As late as 1934 Kandinsky acknowledged his debt to Jawlensky.

However, Kandinsky was not just interested in the formal qualities of modern French painting. His writings suggest that some of its theoretical implications appealed to him. Kandinsky's first important statement about French art appears in his fifth 'Letter from Munich' written in 1911 for the St Petersburg journal *Apollon*, which had begun publication in 1909. In this 'Letter' Kandinsky expressed his enthusiasm for Manet's paintings which he had seen in an exhibition held at the Moderne Galerie Thannhauser in spring 1910. The extract repays close reading:

> The whole atmosphere of the room seemed permeated with an all-devouring, fantastic, superhuman, elemental talent. Everything I dislike about this kind of art was forgotten . . . I was conquered by this boundless, objectless love of painting. Yes, objectless! . . . This was how it appeared to me in the very first moments. Manet lived, looked, saw. Some chance appearance would persistently, peremptorily capture his glance (not his soul) – a woman with black hair, a *vendeuse* at the bar . . . and so on . . . and immediately he would become slave to that appearance, so that it would evolve within him until, inevitably, inescapably, it would be repeated upon the canvas. Not that this repetition was purely mechanical, of course, nor did it by any means involve fixing *every* aspect of reality. His stature, his greatness, lay precisely in his ability to select from the merely accidental that which is artistically necessary. For Manet this necessity consisted almost exclusively in what was pictorially necessary . . . I said 'almost'. When I paused to consider this 'almost', there appeared before my eyes with unexpected clarity the link that exists between the objectless song of Manet and that definite *internal necessity* which . . . has been explored by no less outstanding talents – Cézanne, Van Gogh and Gauguin, and later pre-eminently, by Matisse and Picasso . . . Slowly, one thing has led to another. And slowly, the inwardly necessary has assumed and continues to assume preponderance over the outwardly necessary, just as throughout the whole of our youthful culture, the spiritual is beginning to outweigh the purely material. Slowly, but inexorably, conscious creativity comes into its own, and with it the elements that will constitute the already advancing composition of the future: a kind of composition that is pure, untrammelled, exclusively pictorial, based on evident laws of combination, of movement, of the consonance and dissonance of form, of line and colour.
>
> (Kandinsky, 'Letters from Munich' V, October–November 1910, *Kandinsky, Complete Writings on Art*, page 79.)

Kandinsky's account of his reactions to Manet's paintings is interesting, particularly in the context of this course. On one level it confirms his interest in various ideas which we have now come to identify with the development of Modernism – 'objectless art', 'chance appearance', the 'artistically' and 'inwardly necessary', the 'spiritual', the 'material', and so on. He even emphasized some of these words typographically in the text. Interestingly this text reveals Kandinsky's evident confusion about the compatibility of these issues which were integral to the developing theory of Modernism. In the introduction we saw how some critics tried to reconcile notions of 'chance appearance' and 'objectless art' by implying that the significance of images could be overlooked. But the link Kandinsky draws between Manet's selecting something 'artistically' or 'inwardly necessary', and his subservience to 'chance appearances', for example, is even more obscure, and harder to grasp. Kandinsky's interpretation of Manet's paintings is unclear, and, at times, apparently paradoxical.

Are there any links that can be drawn between Kandinsky's seemingly disparate interests? His concern with contemporary French painting, the *World of Art* and *Jugendstil* may, for example, have seemed to you to be incompatible, but as far as Kandinsky was concerned they shared very specific characteristics.

In 1911, a year after his Manet review, Kandinsky published an article entitled 'Whither the "New" Art?', in the *Odessa News*. In it he returned to the theme of the contrast between the Realists' conception of art (which I outlined briefly, page 11), and that of the Symbolists. Like their European counterparts (see Radiovision programme 7) the Russian Symbolists who were associated with the *World of Art*, often embraced Idealist philosophical notions (see pages 28 ff). In very crude terms, the Symbolists maintained the existence of a 'spiritual' reality, beyond the world of immediate physical reality. They considered it desirable to try to cast aside those ties which bound them to what they thought of as the material world, and seek a kind of spiritual, or fundamental truth. They thought art could play a part in this spiritual elevation, and conceived of it as a vehicle of transcendence which could awaken or stimulate spiritual awareness in observers. Precisely because they held these ideas, their art, unlike that of the Realists, was free from any concern to record descriptively the details of everyday life. The Realists criticized the Symbolists' work for being 'affected and unintelligible'. Kandinsky, on the other hand, thought this 'unintelligibility' laudable:

> While rejecting any material, tangible 'content', these [Symbolist] artists could neither see nor find a new 'content' (i.e. an immaterial one, possessed only by art and effused only by it). Hence, they declared any content to be unartistic and alien to art. Art does not have an aim, they said; it has an aim unto itself, *L'art pour l'art* [art for its own sake].
>
> This very statement contained the seedling of the salvation and liberation of art from its servility to material: once art is self-sufficient, it must concentrate on itself, above all, must attend to itself and *its own means of expression*.
>
> Art, as it were, turns its back on life (so it appears) and turns to its own arsenal. In this arsenal (which had fallen into virtual oblivion), it finds its own means of expression, and is endowed with a titanic strength and a spiritual resonance not to be found in any other field.
>
> (Kandinsky, 'Whither the "New" Art?', 1911, *Kandinsky. Complete Writings on Art*, page 100)

▶ Please re-read the extracts from Kandinsky's 'Whither the "New" Art?' and 'Letter from Munich' (page 26). What characteristics does Kandinsky attribute to both the Russian and the French art he discussed? What does this suggest to you about the nature of his interests in art in general? ◀

▷ Kandinsky aired many of the same ideas in both articles – ideas which probably reflected his interests in general: the view that art could be without 'tangible content' (in the context of 'Whither the "New" Art?' he was probably alluding to the narrative, and often sentimental 'content' of the Wanderers' paintings), and that painting could be autonomous, inherently expressive, and somehow 'spiritual', as though this constituted an alternative to 'content'. By implication he set up an opposition between art and 'life', or material reality.

Kandinsky evidently thought it possible to interpret quite different kinds of art – for example, that produced by the *World of Art* artists, *Jugendstil* designers, Manet, Monet and Matisse – equally well in relation to these ideas. It is easy to see how. He could have conceived of the medieval themes depicted by artists like Bilibin as representing an alternative to the contemporaneous 'content' of the Realists' paintings, and his understanding of the *World of Art* and *Jugendstil* artists' concern with decorative qualities might have contributed to his notion of an autonomous art. His tendency to interpret art according to his own highly idiosyncratic theoretical model presumably accounts for his unusual interpretation of Manet's work.

Given Kandinsky's adoption of these various ideas, it is not hard to see how he came to think of producing 'abstract' paintings. I will be discussing this point in Part 2 of this block. But why should Kandinsky have been receptive to these ideas in particular? What kinds of circumstances caused them to take so firm a hold on his imagination? In order to answer that question we need to look at contemporary philosophical beliefs, particularly those held by the intellectual milieu within which Kandinsky moved. ◁

Kandinsky's philosophical and mystical beliefs

As Belinda Thomson pointed out in Block III ('Symbolism' pages 26 ff), philosophical Idealism attracted many adherents at the end of the nineteenth century, particularly among artists, writers and composers. One of the most influential Idealist philosophers was Arthur Schopenhauer, whose treatise, *The World as Will and Representation* was originally published in 1818. His ideas particularly appealed to many artists and writers from the mid-nineteenth century onwards. There is evidence to show that the painter Marc and Schoenberg the composer, both associated with the *Blaue Reiter*, were indebted to Schopenhauer. Although Kandinsky never specifically refers to the philosopher in his writings many of the ideas that characterize his theory of art are implicit in Schopenhauer's thought.

Idealist philosophy is founded on the assumption that in addition to the immediate, physical or material world, there is another 'world' of 'ideas'. It is presumed that the material world is a shadow or a 'representation' of the 'world' of 'ideas'.

According to Schopenhauer, man's relation to the world is determined by what he calls the 'Will', an inexorable force which not only governs all our actions, impulses and ambitions but the way we 'represent' the world to ourselves. Because of our 'Will' we can never see the world as it really is, we 'represent' phenomena and events to ourselves in those terms which best suit our own immediate self-interest. The one way we might free ourselves from the ties that bind us to the 'Will' is through art and aesthetic contemplation. Part of Schopenhauer's appeal to artists lay precisely in the fact that art was central to his philosophical system.

Schopenhauer proposed that when we study objects aesthetically we lose all sense of our normal identity and our purposeful, 'Will'-ful behaviour. Rather than concerning ourselves with the functions of objects, we look to their 'purely abstract qualities' – their 'harmony' and their 'beauty'. In doing so we become what the philosopher called the 'pure "Will"-less subject of contemplation.' As such, and only as such, we become capable of perceiving the world as undistorted 'Idea' rather than distorted 'Representation'.

Schopenhauer thought that this state of pure aesthetic contemplation was, in principle, accessible to everyone. But he distinguished the artist, more particularly the composer, by the ability to record and convey his or her experience through art. In *The World as Will and Representation* he described how the composer 'reveals the innermost essence of the world, pronouncing the most profound truths in a language his reason cannot understand, drawing, like a galvanized sleepwalker, conclusions as to things of which, waking, he has no conception'. (This very quotation was cited in the *Blaue Reiter* Almanac.) It was, therefore, within the artist's or composer's power to enable observers to perceive 'Ideas'.

Of all the arts, Schopenhauer considered music the 'highest', being the best medium within which to express metaphysical truth. He argued that music was the only art not bound by some kind of function, the way painting was by its function of representation, for example. Nor was it bound to material things, as art is to paint and canvas, or architecture to stone. Schopenhauer thought paintings which depicted objects with excessive fidelity to nature were likely to reinforce man's normal 'Will'-ful manner of looking at the world, rather than elevating him to the realm of 'Will'-less contemplation.

Idealist thought was clearly crucial for the development of Kandinsky's ideas. It constituted a philosophical system within which certain notions were implicit and were presented in a specific relationship to each other, providing, as it were, a model which Kandinsky might emulate. It also seemed to him to justify notions like that of the artist as an intuitive genius creating works which would, by definition, be generally incomprehensible. It also seemed to encourage artists to empha-size the formal elements in their work, rather than qualities of resemblance. Ideas like these typified Symbolist thinking. The issues they raised were, as we have seen, central to the Russian Symbolist/Realist debate.

Surprisingly, Kandinsky's ideas are rarely considered in relation to Idealism. However, it has been claimed that he was indebted to Theosophical teachings and that his work should be seen within that context.

Figure 13 Photograph of Madame Blavatsky, 1834. Mary Evans Picture Library, London.

The Theosophical Society was one of the many esoteric spiritual and occult movements founded in Europe towards the end of the nineteenth century. It was founded in 1875 by the Russian Helena Petrovona Blavatsky (Figure 13). The Theosophists believed in a deeper spiritual reality with which man could communi-cate through states transcending his normal consciousness. They also claimed that by the beginning of the twentieth century a new spiritual epoch would begin, and by 'the twenty-first century, this earth will be a paradise by comparison with what it is now' (quoted by Kandinsky in *On the Spiritual in Art*).

By the end of the nineteenth century many European intellectuals had become interested in Theosophy. It seemed an essentially optimistic movement, providing hope and solace to those dissatisfied by changes in modern society, like the develop-ment of technology and urbanization, and to those made uncertain about the state of their knowledge of the world as a consequence of recent discoveries, like Ein-stein's Theory of Relativity and Planck's Quantum Theory. By 1910 its popularity had spread to Russia. Particular interest was aroused by its teachings about the coming of a new age. It was as if Theosophy heralded a kind of spiritual change, somehow analogous to the social and political concepts of change which had re-sulted in the abortive Revolution of 1905.

There is evidence that Kandinsky was familiar with Theosophical teaching. Members of the circles within which he mixed in Munich were interested in Theosophy; his and Münter's library contained several articles and books on the subject although it has been suggested that most of these actually belonged to Münter. He is reported to have attended a lecture by Rudolf Steiner, then Secretary of the German branch in 1908. He even refers specifically to Theosophy and Mme Blavatsky in his 1911 book *On the Spiritual in Art*. We can, however, only speculate how Theosophy might have influenced his thinking (see page 39). But we should note that there are certain similarities between Theosophy and Idealism; for example, the Idealist notion of the artist as a perceiver of 'Ideas', and the theosophical mystical concept of a 'seer' or a magical practitioner aware of invisible forces like 'auras'. Later in the block I will be looking at how critics associated these mystical notions with Kandinsky's work.

In this part of the block I have tried to show you the kinds of ideas Kandinsky was open to during his years in Munich, particularly ideas about 'primitivism', and the 'spiritual', and that these constitute part of the context within which we should consider his development of 'abstract' painting. In Part 2 I want to consider how some of these ideas might have become incorporated within Kandinsky's thinking, and how, in practical terms, he set about constructing his paintings in relation to them.

2 Kandinsky: theory and art practice

Kandinsky's theory

The fullest theoretical statement Kandinsky made before 1914 is in *On the Spiritual in Art*, a book of about 35,000 words. *On the Spiritual in Art* was based on notes Kandinsky made from the time he arrived in Munich in 1896. The typescript is dated 1909, but the book was published in 1911, appearing in time for the first *Blaue Reiter* exhibition. By 1912, *On the Spiritual in Art* had been through three editions, a fourth was planned for 1914, but the outbreak of war prevented publication. *On the Spiritual in Art* has subsequently been through numerous editions in various languages, and has been regarded as one of the most influential books on art theory published this century.

On the Spiritual in Art opens with Kandinsky's assertion that works of art reflect the spirit of the time and society in which they are produced, an observation frequently made in contemporary German writings about art (see Block IV, Part 2b). Kandinsky characterized contemporary society as having been corrupted by what he called 'the long epoch of materialism', which had in his opinion, rendered modern life spiritually bankrupt: '. . . men place exclusive value upon outward success, concern themselves only with material goods . . . Purely spiritual values are at best underestimated, or go generally unnoticed.' Kandinsky proposed that society might be divided into different groups according to the extent to which they appeared to him to be preoccupied by 'materialist' concerns. He describes this structure by analogy with a triangle or pyramid divided horizontally. Kandinsky thought the inhabitants of the largest and lowest group the most 'materialist'. Because of their views about economics, he categorizes them as 'socialists . . . supporting their "convictions" with a wealth of quotations . . . from Marx's *Capital*, and much more'; scientifically, they are 'positivists' and in terms of art they are 'naturalists', who thought they were thus licensed in Tolstoi's terms (see page 15) to 'draw and paint everything'. Theirs were the kinds of paintings which could be found by the thousand at exhibitions like the annual *Glaspalast* shows (see page 16) representing:

> . . . pieces of 'nature' . . . animals in light and shadow, standing at the edge of the water, drinking the water, lying in the grass, next to them a crucifixion of Christ, portrayed by a painter who does not believe in Christ, flowers, human forms sitting, standing, walking . . . many naked women (often seen foreshortened from behind), apples and silver dishes, a portrait of Privy Councillor So-and-So, the evening sun, a woman in pink, flying ducks . . .
>
> (Kandinsky, *On the Spiritual in Art, Kandinsky. Complete Writings on Art,* page 129)

Kandinsky objected to the way such paintings were appreciated: 'Connoisseurs admire the "technique" (as one admires a tightrope walker), enjoy the *"peinture"* (just as one enjoys pâté)', and he was disparaging about the kind of artist who painted such works intending to make money from them:

> His aim becomes the satisfaction of his own ambition and greed. Instead of a close collaboration among artists, there is a scramble for these rewards . . . Hatred,

bias, factions, jealousy and intrigue are the consequences of this purposeless,
materialistic art.

(Kandinsky, *On the Spiritual in Art, Kandinsky. Complete Writings*, page 130)

Kandinsky, of course, was in the fortunate position of not needing to sell paintings
to earn his living (see page 20). He considered that the inhabitants of the 'higher
echelons' included 'professional intellectuals' (philosophers and physicists) who had
started casting doubts on the nature of matter itself, 'which was yesterday the basis
of everything and upon which the whole universe was supported' (see page 29).
Inhabitants of still higher 'classes' are characterized by the fact that they look for an
alternative to the 'materialist' view of reality, one based on 'eternal truths', like that
promised by the Theosophists.

Kandinsky insisted that art had a part to play in the evolution of that undefined
'utopian state', heralding that 'change' he had identified in 'Whither the "New"
Art?':

> A general interest in abstraction is being reborn, both in the superficial form of the
> movement towards the spiritual, and in the forms of occultism, spiritualism, mon-
> ism, the 'new' Christianity, theosophy, and religion in its broadest sense.
>
> (Kandinsky, 'Whither the "New" Art?', *Kandinsky. Complete Writings*, page 101)

He envisaged the artist's function as feeding 'the obstinate cartload of humanity'
with 'spiritual bread', a task well within his capabilities since, according to Kandinsky, the 'true' artist stands 'at the apex of the topmost division of the triangle'.
In other words, Kandinsky envisaged art as a spiritual mission:

> . . . without fail, there appears among us a man like the rest of us in every way,
> but who conceals within himself the secret, inborn power of 'vision'.
>
> He sees and points. Sometimes he would gladly be rid of this higher gift, which
> is often a heavy cross for him to bear. But he cannot. Through mockery and
> hatred, he continues to drag the heavy cartload of struggling humanity, getting
> stuck amid the stones, ever onward and upward.
>
> (Kandinsky, *On the Spiritual in Art, Kandinsky. Complete Writings*, page 131)

If, as Kandinsky implied, 'naturalistic' art resulted from an empathetic relationship
between man and the material world, the kind of art he was proposing as an alternative could be accounted for in terms of what Worringer had described in 1908 as
'the outcome of a great inner unrest inspired in man by the phenomena of the
outside world [which] in a religious respect . . . corresponds to a strongly transcen-
dental tinge to all notions' (Reader, Text 25). The kinds of function Kandinsky
envisaged for art were analogous to those Schopenhauer attributed to music, that it
could reveal what he called the 'innermost essence of the world'. As you will recall,
Schopenhauer had proposed the idea that music could express this precisely because
of its lack of material boundaries and its emancipation from narrative, or any need
to represent objects.

As early as 1904, in a letter to Münter, Kandinsky had expressed his dislike for
what he called 'obtrusive content' in art.

> To me, obtrusive content is neither beautiful nor noble nor delicate . . . At first
> sight, some things must have the effort of incomprehensibility. Thereafter the
> beauty will come to the fore, and only then, to the sensitive observer, the inner
> content . . . This content, however, must never be too clear and too simple; the
> more possibilities for interpretation through fantasy the better.
>
> (Kandinsky, letter to Münter, 31 January 1904. Quoted in Roethel, 'Introduction'
> to the catalogue, *Wassily Kandinsky. Painting on Glass*, 1966, page 12.)

By the time he wrote *On the Spiritual in Art*, Kandinsky evidently thought something very like Schopenhauer's conception of music provided the kind of model he
wanted to emulate in art.

An artist who sees that the imitation of natural appearances, however artistic, is not for him – the kind of creative artist who wants to, and has to, express his own *inner* world – sees with envy how naturally and easily such goals can be attained in music, the least material of the arts today.

(Kandinsky, *On the Spiritual in Art, Kandinsky. Complete Writings*, page 154)

He not only wanted painting to be recognized as sharing the same lofty spiritual status as that which Schopenhauer attributed to music, he also wanted painting's means of expression, its 'language', to be somehow analogous to that of music. It is understandable, he wrote in *On the Spiritual in Art*, if the artist turns towards music and tries to find 'the same means in his own art. Hence the current search for rhythm in painting, for mathematical, abstract construction, the value placed today upon the repetition of colour-tones, the way colours are set in motion, etc.'

The idea that an analogy existed between musical and pictorial language was frequently aired in writings about art from the middle of the nineteenth century (see Hamilton, page 303) and from the end of the nineteenth century many artists and critics took it for granted. In *On the Spiritual in Art* Kandinsky suggested that colours and forms might function as a language in the same way as he presumed musical notes and structures did in expressing ideas. Consequently, he was particularly interested in the 'expressive' possibilities of colour, and two chapters in his book are specifically entitled 'The Effect of Colour' and 'The Language of Forms and Colours'.

▶ Please read 'The Effect of Colour' (Chipp, pages 152–5).

1   What kinds of questions about colour interested Kandinsky?

2   Are they the same kinds of questions addressed in other colour theories you have encountered elsewhere, for instance Chevreul's (see Hamilton, page 51 and, in connection with Seurat, *Supplementary Documents* III. 2, pages 17–18.)? What is the difference?

3   Can you suggest why Kandinsky was interested in the particular issues he addressed? To answer this you may find it useful to look back over the section on 'Kandinsky's philosophical and mystical beliefs' (page 28). ◀

▷ At times in *On the Spiritual in Art* Kandinsky's observations about colour have a certain amount in common with other, conventional colour theories, but in 'The Effect of Colour' what he is proposing is a rather different notion of colour to that proposed in the 'scientific' theory of Chevreul. He is concerned with colours giving rise to psychological, rather than physiological effects. Kandinsky's philosophical interests partly account for this. His commitment to Idealism and to the idea of 'the spiritual' was antithetical to nineteenth-century materialism and positivism. Schopenhauer had proposed that the kinds of understanding gleaned from science and art were incompatible. He disdained science and rational processes because he thought they could only provide a limited account of why particular phenomena exist 'at a particular time, in a particular place, under certain conditions, as a result of certain causes, producing certain effects'. At the time of writing 'The Effect of Colour' Kandinsky probably thought that colour theories like Chevreul's were thus limited.

There were precedents for what we might call a 'spiritual' theory of colour; Goethe's *Theory of Colours* originally published in 1810, for example, which was very influential in the early years of the twentieth century. Goethe proposed an essentially unscientific theory which attributed to colours, among other things, 'moral' or metaphorical effects. Goethe's complete scientific writings were republished between 1884 and 1897 in the series *Kürschners Deutsche National-Literatur*, which was edited and introduced by Rudolf Steiner, later the Secretary to the

German branch of the Theosophical Society. From about this time onwards echoes of Goethe's colour system recur throughout theosophical discussions of colour. Kandinsky's notions of the effects of colour need to be seen within this context.

Kandinsky asserts that colours have what he calls a 'physical' effect on the spectator, stimulating the eye 'as the tongue is titillated by a spicy dish'. But he thought that colours can also exert psychological effects, and, by extension, that they possess their own 'internal meaning', something felt only by the more highly developed and 'sensitive soul'. This may be due to the spectator associating the colour with a particular object or experience, in the way 'red may cause a sensation analogous to that created by flame'. On the other hand, the experience of a given colour may in 'some particularly sensitive' observers stimulate the response of another sense organ, an experience known as synaesthesia. This is another notion often aired in writings about colour from the end of the nineteenth century onwards. By way of evidence Kandinsky cites the extremely dubious case of the Dresden doctor who reported that one of his patients, 'an exceptionally sensitive person', could not eat a certain sauce without tasting blue. Such ideas, of course, imply that colours can mean different things to different people, therefore suggesting that colour is an inadequate means of communication (see page 51).

Kandinsky also proposed that colours could stimulate a physical reaction in the observer, and referred to 'chromotherapy' – an experimental form of 'treatment' in which exposure to particular colours was used to alleviate mental distress, in the belief that they possess therapeutic value. Just to make sure there was no misunderstanding, Kandinsky added the following footnote to his account of the effects of colour: 'All these assertions are the result of empirical-spiritual experience, and are not based on any positive-scientific system'. ◁

Kandinsky's conception of 'The Effect of Colour' had obvious implications for his developing theory of art, and of an 'abstract' visual language. If, as he suggested, colours did have psychological or associative effects, they could not be considered as purely formal elements. He thought of them as 'expressive', and, one could say, as representative of certain ideas. It should be clear that Kandinsky's notion of 'abstraction' cannot be easily made to conform to the polarity between 'abstraction' and 'representation' suggested by some of the critics whose writings we looked at in the introduction. For Kandinsky, 'abstract' certainly did *not* mean stripped of reference to ideas.

In his attempt to make a case for the 'expressive' function of what were usually considered to be the 'formal' elements of painting, Kandinsky also alleged elsewhere in *On the Spiritual in Art* that 'Form itself, even if completely abstract, resembling geometric form, has an inner sound, is a spiritual being . . .'. He suggested that in conjunction with other forms, this 'inner sound' might become 'differentiated, receiving additional nuances, but remaining in essence unchangeable'. As you will realize from reading extracts from Kandinsky's writings, his conception of 'inner sound' is crucial to an understanding of his theory of pictorial language. It is probably best described by analogy with another of his theories – his theory of language.

Kandinsky thought that words, like forms, possessed what he called their own 'resonance' or 'inner sound'. This 'inner sound', he writes,

> arises partly – perhaps principally – from the object for which the word serves as a name. But when the object itself is not seen, but only its name is heard, an abstract conception arises in the mind of the listener, a dematerialized object that at once conjures up a vibration in the 'heart'. The *green* or *yellow* or *red tree* as it stands in the meadow is merely a material occurrence, an accidental materialization of the form of that tree we feel within ourselves when we hear the word *tree*.
>
> (Kandinsky, *On the Spiritual in Art, Kandinsky. Complete Writings on Art*, page 147)

However, Kandinsky also thought that words had expressive potential. He suggested the repetition of a word might 'lead not only to the growth of the inner sound, but also brings to light still other, unrealized spiritual qualities of the word', making it lose 'its external sense as a name':

> In this way, even the sense of the word as an abstract indication of the object is forgotten, and only the pure *sound* of the word remains. We may also, perhaps, unconsciously, hear this 'pure' sound at the same time as we perceive the real, or subsequently, the abstract object. In the latter case, however, this pure sound comes to the fore and exercises a direct influence upon the soul.
>
> (Kandinsky, *On the Spiritual in Art, Kandinsky. Complete Writings* page 147)

Kandinsky suggested that this theory opened up great possibilities for future literature, possibilities best exemplified by his own poems. Around about 1912 (see Appendix A) Kandinsky published an album of poems entitled *Klänge* (*Sounds*). As the title of the album suggests the sounds of the words used were fundamental to the composition of the poems.

▶ One of the poems entitled 'Sehen' ('Seeing') is reproduced in the *Supplementary Documents* (VII.3). Please read it several times to get a 'feel' of the words. ◀

As you will see from the English translation the poem functions on two levels. On one hand, the sounds of the words determine the structure and the rhythms of the poem. In this respect it could be compared to the Russian Futurist poets' trans-rational experiments (see Block VIII) and those written by the Zurich Dadaists (discussed in Block XI). On the other hand, the meaning of the words is important too.

Kandinsky's literary innovations seemed to him to have clear theoretical implications for painting. If literature could work on two levels, as conventional narrative and as 'pure sound', why shouldn't visual form work in the same way, as a type of expressive utterance freed from specific reference?

Some critics, including those we looked at in the introduction, were convinced Kandinsky had painted what they thought of as an 'abstract' painting by 1910. There is no suggestion in Kandinsky's own writings of 1910 that he thought he had done so. It was only in 1914 when he made notes for the proposed alterations to *On the Spiritual in Art* that he mentioned the possibility of 'abstract' art for the first time (see Appendix B). Unfortunately he fails to cite a single example of this 'abstract' painting. What seems to me to be interesting about *On the Spiritual in Art* is that it reveals Kandinsky floundering. However much the notion of an 'abstract' or rather 'non-objective' art may have appealed to him, he apparently doubted the practical viability of his theoretical ideas: 'What seemed so easy just would not come in practice'. In the second edition of *On the Spiritual in Art*, published in 1912, two years after the Modernist critics would have us believe Kandinsky had already painted the 'First Abstract Watercolour' (see page 44) he was, in his own opinion, '. . . still bound to the outward appearance of nature'.

Although Kandinsky believed forms and colours were, theoretically, 'expressive', he was only too well aware that to turn to a mode of painting based only on 'geometric forms' would be to reduce the 'expressive' potential of his work. He even acknowledged that his observations about the 'Effects of Colours' were 'not universal' (Chipp, page 153). He clearly did not want his art, which he considered a vehicle for the communication of profound spiritual truths – the highest function of art – to be mistaken for, or compared with, a meaningless ornament (see Appendix B, Extract 2, page 56). As one critic had acutely and sarcastically observed in 1910, Kandinsky was 'too good to allow his work to be put on the same level as designers'. Kandinsky thought that the most important function of his paintings was to communicate. In 'Reminiscences' he remembered that at the time of writing *On the Spiritual in Art,* 'I still laboured under the delusion that the viewer confronts the painting with an open soul, and wants to detect an affinity within it'. He realized that 'If the artist and the spectator. . . no longer understand one another, the latter turns his back on the former'. His solution was to retain 'representational' forms, in the same way that he retained words whose meaning was important in his poems:

> Must we not then renounce the object all together, throw it to the winds and instead lay bare the purely abstract? . . . Just as every word spoken (tree, sky, man) awakens an inner vibration, so too does every pictorially represented object. To deprive oneself of the possibility of thus calling up vibrations would be to narrow one's arsenal of expressive means. At least, that is how it is today.
>
> (Kandinsky, 'The Language of Colours and Forms', *On the Spiritual in Art, Kandinsky. Complete Writings,* page 169)

▶ In the 'Cologne Lecture' of 1914, he explained why he did not want to 'banish objects completely'. Please read Extract 5, Appendix B, page 57, very carefully. ◀

Kandinsky's attitude to 'abstraction' is clearly ambivalent. On the one hand he clearly envisages his goal to be the creation of an 'abstract' work. On the other, he is unwilling to abandon 'representational' forms. More importantly, before 1914 he was, as far as we can see, unable to produce a painting whose forms, be they classified as 'abstract' or 'representational' did not represent something.

Similarly, whatever his account of Manet might have suggested (see page 26), he did not conceive of his 'abstract' work as the logical conclusion of a longstanding interest in purely formal values. His view of 'abstraction' was, then, in many respects, *incompatible* with those interpretations attached to his work by many subsequent critics. (Interestingly, the 'Cologne Lecture' in which Kandinsky so clearly pointed to his concern with 'material forms' was not published until 1957, by which time the Modernist view of Kandinsky was already well established — see Appendix B.)

Kandinsky's paintings

In the introduction to this block, I suggested that there were problems in trying to see what Kandinsky's so-called 'abstract' paintings represented without knowing anything of the context in which they were created. Having now looked at some of the circumstances which governed their production we should hopefully be better equipped to consider them.

Some of the critical accounts we looked at in the introduction suggested that Kandinsky's 'abstract' pictures developed from his 'representational' work, implying that they were painted later. But the artist's own record of the pictures he produced shows that he was painting highly 'abstracted' and obviously 'representational' works, like the *Landscape with Two Poplars* (**Pl. VII. 4**), at the same time. The presence of such works in Kandinsky's *œuvre* must have caused consternation among those later critics set on tracing the linear development of 'abstraction', which they accounted for in terms of artists' decreased interest in 'representation' and increased interest in formal elements. Some, like Roger Fry, disregarded the presence of subject matter in such paintings, describing them in the same terms as they would a more 'abstracted' work. In his review of Kandinsky's paintings at the AAA (see page 8) Fry described his 1912 *Landscape with Two Poplars*, as he had *Improvisation No. 30* (**Col.pl.VII.3**), as 'pure visual music'. In the catalogue *Cubism and Abstract Art,* Barr tried to cope with this problem by describing the landscape as 'less abstract' than the 'more abstract' *Improvisation No. 30* of the following year. More generally, the existence within Kandinsky's *œuvre* of works with such a high degree of resemblance after he was supposed to have painted the 'First Abstract

Watercolour', has simply been ignored. Is Kandinsky's ambivalent attitude towards 'abstract' art only discernible in comparing the different kinds of paintings he chose to paint? Might it not also be a characteristic of individual paintings?

In order to try and answer that question we are going to look at a picture Kandinsky painted in 1911, the same year that *On the Spiritual in Art* was published, *Composition 4* (**Col.pl.VII.7**). One might think a painting with such a title would be one in which the artist was primarily concerned with the formal effects of colours and forms. The title, *Composition 4* implies that the painting lacks conventional subject matter and that Kandinsky thought this painting somehow analagous to a musical 'composition'. But is it as simple as that? In 1913 Kandinsky published a statement about that painting, written in 1911, which you will find reproduced in the *Supplementary Documents*, VII.1.

▶ Please read Kandinsky's essay *'Composition 4'*, and look very carefully at the reproduction of the painting (**Col.pl.VII.7**). How would you characterize his attitude towards 'abstraction' in relation to this painting? Can you identify any resemblance to specific objects in the painting? ◀

▷ In his essay, Kandinsky devotes considerable attention to the 'effects' created by different colours and forms in the painting; the contrasts between the formal components of the painting; the way in which colour 'disrupts' the outlines of forms, and the compositional arrangement of the painting. But he also points to the representation of specific objects in the picture; entangled horses, reclining figures, a battle, a castle and lances – motifs which he might otherwise have been unaware of, and which were evidently important to Kandinsky. In a letter written to a friend more than sixteen years after the painting was completed, Kandinsky commented that 'in this painting, one still sees the remnants of objects: Cossacks, lances, city walls, horses'. He also observed: 'In 1911 no one was able to recognize the objective element in this picture, which is very characteristic of the visual attitudes of that time' (see page 45).

Although Kandinsky was willing to acknowledge that there were objects depicted in his painting, he was not prepared to explain his works in terms of such subject-matter. In fact he was in general extremely reluctant to discuss the element of resemblance in his paintings. ◁

In *On the Spiritual in Art* Kandinsky had defined an 'improvisation' as the kind of painting created 'chiefly unconsciously', and 'for the most part, suddenly'. He described its content as 'an expression of events of an inner character'. But in a letter written in 1913 to the collector, Arthur Jerome Eddy, Kandinsky referred to his *Improvisation No. 30* (**Col.pl.VII.3**) as *Cannons*, a name which does suggest the presence of subject-matter in the painting. Indeed two cannons are quite clearly depicted in the lower right hand of the painting. But Kandinsky catagorically denied that the painting was *about* cannons. He told Eddy that 'the presence of cannons in the picture could probably be explained by the constant war-talk which had been going on throughout the year'. 'But', he stipulated, 'I did not intend to give a representation of war'. He claimed the designation *Cannons* was 'selected by me for my own use' and that it was 'not conceived as indicating the "contents" of the picture. These contents are indeed what the spectator lives or feels while under the effect of the form and colour combinations of the picture'.

These statements suggest that Kandinsky was as ambivalent about the 'abstract' nature of individual paintings as he was about 'abstract' art in his theoretical writings, and that he was uncertain about how painting might function as a vehicle for expression through the 'abstract power of colour', or by the impressions created by recognizable motifs. Precisely because of this we should treat Kandinsky's statements with a certain amount of caution, particularly those statements in which he is non-committal about the part resemblance plays in his paintings. For however unclear Kandinsky was about it, he obviously saw representation – including representation by resemblance – as being of crucial importance to his work, especially considering his belief in its 'messianic' function. Certainly some kinds of subject-matter must have seemed to him eminently more suitable than others. He admitted to retaining references to objects in his paintings precisely because he believed that recognition played an essential role in the dialogue between artist and observer. It follows that we must be able to identify the iconography of his 'abstract' works if we are going to begin to understand them, though, of course, that is only one aspect of their means of representation. What I want to do in the following paragraphs is to consider some of the motifs Kandinsky used.

How might we go about this? As I suggested in the introduction to this block (page 6), we cannot recognize Kandinsky's images by looking at specific paintings in isolation. As we have already seen, the artist deliberately intended to mystify the spectators by 'dissolving' those images, thus making them less easily recognizable. We know that by the time he started work on a canvas he had already decided how the 'abstracted' images would appear. This is made clear by the series of photographs Münter took over four days in 1913 when Kandinsky was at work on his *Composition 7* (Pls VII.22–25; see also Hamilton, page 212). Sometimes preliminary studies for paintings present the imagery in a more legible, less abstracted form than the final painting. These help us, for example, with the 1913 oil painting, *Small Pleasures* (Col.pl.VII.8).

Before starting work on *Small Pleasures*, Kandinsky made a glass painting (Pl.VII.26), a study for that glass painting (Pl. VII. 27) and a smaller oil painting entitled *Improvisation 21a* (Pl.VII.28). In the glass painting we can identify images of a large sun; an embracing couple standing at an angle; two hills, each surmounted by a citadel; three horsemen galloping up a hillside; a black cloud with a white centre, and three figures in a rowing boat.

A careful comparison between the oil (Col.pl.VII.8) and the glass painting shows how Kandinsky 'dissolved' these images. He simplified the three horsemen and their riders to linear constructions. The embracing couple at the bottom left is almost unrecognizable, the woman being almost totally 'dissolved' and the man's trunk indicated by two tapering black lines. The hills are distinct, but the citadel is reduced to an almost transparent construction of geometrical forms. Other motifs like the dark cloud in the top right and the rowing boat below are relatively unchanged.

Merely recognizing these images, however, does not inform us about their significance. As I mentioned earlier in the context of the discussion about *The Motley Life* (page 25), Kandinsky often used the same images in different contexts and combinations. Looking at those may tell us something about the significance Kandinsky attached to particular images. Images of the embracing couple, the citadel and the simultaneously dark and light sky occur in a glass painting of 1911, *All Saints 1* (Col.pl.VII.9); the horse and rider, the hill and citadel occur in the badly damaged glass painting, *Large Resurrection* 1911 (Pl.VII.29), its related watercolour (Pl.VII.30), and woodcut from *Klänge (Sounds)* (Col.pl.VII.10). They also appear in the woodcut vignette for the title page of *On the Spiritual in Art* (Pl.VII.31). The rowers recur in Kandinsky's work of the period – *Improvisation 26 (The Rowers)* (Pl.VII.32); the woodcut for the back cover of the *Blaue Reiter* (Pl.VII.33) combined with the image of the rider, and in the lower left corner of *Composition 6* (subtitled *The Deluge*) (Pl.VII.35) and *Composition 7* (Pls VII.22–25 and Hamilton, page 212). All these images occur in numerous other works.

The majority of these works were, as some of their titles suggest, concerned with apocalyptic and eschatological themes, in other words, themes that were particularly appropriate for the kind of painting which Kandinsky proposed would advance 'the new spiritual realm . . . the epoch of great spirituality'. In *On the Spiritual in Art* he had, for example, used the image of the citadel with toppling towers, and the darkened sun to suggest how those 'higher', 'spiritual' divisions of the 'triangle' were threatened by the 'darkness' of 'materialism':

> If we climb still higher, we see even greater confusion, as if in a great city, built solidly according to all architectural and mathematical rules, that is suddenly shaken by a mighty force. The people who live in such a division indeed live in such a spiritual city, where such forces are at work, and with which the spiritual architects and mathematicians have not reckoned. Here, part of the massive wall lies fallen like a house of cards. There, an enormous tower that once reached to the sky, built of many slender, and yet 'immortal' spiritual pinnacles, lies in ruins. The old forgotten cemetery quakes . . . The sun, framed so artistically, shows spots and darkens, and what can replace it in the fight against darkness?
>
> (Kandinsky, 'Spiritual Turning Point', *On the Spiritual in Art, Kandinsky. Complete Writings,* pages 141–142.)

The iconographical significance Kandinsky attached to these images was not of his own devising, but related to contemporary usage. The Theosophist, Rudolf Steiner (Figure 14) in particular used apocalyptic imagery to describe the great cataclysmic event he believed would take place before the advent of the new 'spiritual epoch'

Figure 14 Photograph of Rudolf Steiner, 1916. Bildarchiv Österreichischer Nationalbibliothek, Wien.

39

predicted by him (see page 29):

> The Apocalypse of John prophetically points to the cycle of human evolution lying between the great upheaval upon our earth which the legends of various peoples describe as a flood . . . and that event which we describe as the War of All against All . . . In the epoch between these two events lies everything prophetically referred to in the Apocalypse – that book which reveals to us the beings of past ages in order to show what is to fire our will and our impulses for the future.
>
> (Rudolf Steiner, *Die Thesophie an der Hand der Apokalypse,* 1908; Quoted after Washton Long, *Kandinsky. The Development of an Abstract Style*, 1980, page 28.)

Kandinsky also associated these particular images with primitive art, as can be seen from some of the reproductions he included in the *Blaue Reiter* almanac (see page 22 and RV 14), for example, the detail of the toppling tower in the German medieval woodcut from the Nuremberg Bible of 1483 (**Pl. VII.34**). He would have also associated them with the kinds of images used in Russian *lubki*, for instance **Pl. VII.7**, as well as illustrations of scenes from 'The Revelation of St John' (**Pl. VII.6**).

One reason for Kandinsky being attracted by the idea of 'primitive' art might have been the way it was interpreted in contemporary writings. As we have seen (page 32, and Block IV, page 56), writers like Worringer associated it with ideas of 'transcendence' and 'expressivity'. Kandinsky not only used images derived from 'primitive' art in his work, he also adopted what could be regarded as 'primitive' techniques. In Block IV Gill Perry discussed, in relation to the Brücke, the way in which the woodcut, a medium Kandinsky frequently used (see **Pls VII.31,33**) was considered to have supposedly 'primitive' associations. Kandinsky's practice of glass painting should also be seen in this context. He first encountered *Hinterglasmalerei* (literally, painting on the back of glass) in 1908 when he and Münter began living in Murnau, where the tradition of glass painting still continued. According to her recollections, Münter collected these paintings, which she sometimes copied (**Pl. VII.36**), and urged Kandinsky to work in this medium. The themes of traditional Murnau glass paintings were limited – they usually depicted saints somehow connected with the village or region, such as St George and St Martin (**Pl. VII.37**). Kandinsky often used the images of these particular saints in his work (see **Pls. VII.38** and 39). It is possible he imagined that his adoption of a traditional medium and familiar images would make his work more accessible.

▶ At the beginning of this block I asked you to consider what Kandinsky's *Picture with White Border* resembles? In the subsequent discussion I suggested that we could hardly begin to answer a question like that until we looked at the context within which the picture was painted – in what historical, intellectual and social circumstances it was produced.

Please study the reproduction of the painting again (**Col. pl. VII.1**), the related material – preliminary sketches, and possible source material (**Pls VII.41–47**) – and read Kandinsky's essay on the painting (*Supplementary Documents*, VII.2). Drawing on these and on the background material presented in this block, can you now suggest what the painting might be said to represent (a) in terms of those interests we now identify as characterizing Modernism, and (b) in terms of Kandinsky's own theoretical interests? ◀

▷ Kandinsky's account of the production of *Picture with White Border* suggests that his painting was determined by certain interests, some of which are characteristic of what we now identify as Modernism. He implied, for example, that his painting was the result of 'intuitive' processes, returning several times to the theme of 'creative spontaneity', and to the guidance of his 'inner voice'. Kandinsky's tendency to make such proclamations was beloved by those critics who lent credence to his story (related in 'Reminiscences') that the chance discovery of one of his own paintings standing upside down in the twilight inspired him to consider the possibilities of non-objective painting (see Hamilton, page 208). In his account of *Picture with White Border* Kandinsky also emphasized his concern with the formal qualities of the work. He describes, for example, the effects achieved by applying the paint to the canvas in different ways, the different shapes formed on the canvas, and he discusses what he considers to be the inherent expressivity and the meaning of various colours and forms. His references to the 'feelings' they inspired in him (or rather, which he brought to them) suggest that he conceived of this painting as an object for 'aesthetic contemplation'. He evidently wanted also to emphasize the autonomy of the painting. He was careful not to refer to any specific experiences related to the painting or to any objects represented in it.

The idea that paintings might, or rather should display these kinds of interests relates back to specific interests and developing conventions referred to in Part 1. Kandinsky would have encountered these ideas through his knowledge of Idealism, of contemporary criticism of French painting in particular, of subjective colour theories, etc. We could then say that the painting expresses many of Kandinsky's particular interests and aspirations which are also characteristic of Modernism. This would, however, provide us with a narrow and misleading conception of the painting.

For one thing, Kandinsky's description of his paintings as 'intuitive' and resulting from 'creative spontaneity' is contradictory. The evidence of his preliminary drawings, in which specific images are repeated, abstracted and refined over and over again, suggests that he had preconceived ideas about the painting before starting work on it, and that the whole effect of the work was calculated. The drawings present us with recognizable images: a trumpet-blowing angel at the top right; a St George on horseback armed with a lance in the centre, and a monster in the bottom left. At one stage Kandinsky evidently considered including the image of toppling towers in the painting (see **Pls.VII.42,43**). These were images Kandinsky associated with 'primitive' art – Murnau glass paintings, and Russian folk sculpture, like that reproduced in the *Blaue Reiter* (**Pls.VII.34,37** and **46**). Furthermore, as we have seen, Kandinsky attached particular significance to some of these images which were related to the story of the Apocalypse. In *On the Spiritual* he had used the image of the hydra to suggest 'capitalism', 'materialism' and 'evil'. His 'dissolution' of colours and forms was a deliberate way of severing the connection between his supposedly autonomous painting and literary themes, and it makes clear how he set about 'mystifying' his paintings. ◁

The kind of significance Kandinsky attached to his paintings was overlooked in Modernist interpretations, according to which such 'abstract' works as *Picture with White Border* are, in effect, meaningless, in that they were thought to bear no resemblance to the material world. As you will remember in the introduction I cited Barr, who thought 'abstract' paintings 'impoverished' (page 7). However, as you have seen, by locating Kandinsky's paintings in their historical context, we can begin to understand that they do have a significance of which Modernists fail to take account. Understanding such 'abstract' pictures is not merely a question of recognizing residual iconography, but of understanding the significance of certain forms and practices within their technical, intellectual and historical contexts.

3 Abstraction, Modernism and Kandinsky

In this section I will be looking at contemporary, as well as subsequent critical interpretations of Kandinsky and early abstract art in general. My aim is to see how and why those critics we now identify as Modernists have written about Kandinsky's painting in the way they have; why certain issues seemed important to them, and why they adhered to certain standpoints. I also want to consider how those interpretations contributed to myths that have grown up around Kandinsky in particular, and which have shaped general 'histories' of 'abstract' art. Finally, I want to examine the kinds of problems these interpretations raise.

Critical background to abstract art

In order to understand how artists at the beginning of the twentieth century might have conceived of 'abstraction' we need to look back to the kinds of ideas about 'abstraction' aired by critics from the mid-nineteenth century onwards. Although not specifically calling for an 'abstract' art, they were concerned with similar issues to those which preoccupied 'abstract' painters. In retrospect, one might say that their writings constituted an informal theory of 'abstraction' long before artists started to produce 'abstract' art. We may even be able to ask whether 'abstract' art might have been a response to critical demands.

One theme you will already have encountered in the *Introduction* and elsewhere in the course is that of 'autonomy'. In an article entitled 'Representation, Abstraction and the Absolute in Art', published in the journal, *Arts Magazine* in 1977, the art historian Andrew Kagan suggested that 'by the middle of the nineteenth century the concept of "abstraction" had come to embrace a set of theories which postulated that the medium of art was a complete reality in and for itself, irrespective of any questions of how and what it represented'. The term 'abstraction' was applied to art without regard for its representational or narrative content, critical attention being directed towards the formal arrangement of such elements as colour and form. The following passage, taken from *The Stones of Venice*, written in 1853 by the Victorian critic John Ruskin, is used by Kagan to exemplify this kind of approach (you will encounter the same critic cited in Block XII as putting forward a completely opposite view):

> We are to remember, in the first place, that the arrangement of colours and lines is an art analogous to the composition of music, and entirely independent of the representation of facts. Good colouring does not necessarily convey the image of anything but itself. It consists in certain proportions and arrangements of rays of light, but not to likeness in anything.
>
> The noblest art is an exact unison of the abstract value, with the imitative power of forms and colours. It is the noblest composition, used to express the noblest facts.
>
> (John Ruskin, *The Stones of Venice*, 1894, pages 182–84. Quoted after Kagan, 'Representation, Abstraction and the Absolute in Art', page 136.)

As Hamilton observes, the French writer Baudelaire expressed very similar ideas (page 303).

Ruskin's contemporary, the English critic Phillip Gilbert Hammerton, also wrote about formal value in art, even when he knew it had been arrived at 'by accident'. In his book *Imagination in Landscape Painting*, 1896, he claimed one could

> . . . perceive the most unsuspected relations between colour and form in land-scape, . . . even in accidental combinations of mere pigments, as when Turner got three children to dabble water colours together till he suddenly stopped them at the propitious moment. These researches and exercises may easily be condemned as trifling . . . or there may be a colour art, invented by the imagination, without meaning, exactly as there is a sound music without meaning, or, at least, of which the meaning could not possibly be expressed in any language but its own.
>
> (P. G. Hammerton, *Imagination in Landscape Painting*, 1896. Quoted after E. H. Gombrich, 'The Vogue of Abstract Art', *Meditations on a Hobby Horse,* 1971, pages 147–148.)

It seemed to him that this emphasis on formal arrangements rather than narrative content could be identified with the work of certain contemporary artists. Earlier, in 1868, he had claimed:

> . . . [the Impressionists] . . . are beginning to express contempt for all art which in any way depends on the interests of the subject . . . Painting . . . should in their view offer nothing but its own merchandise. And the special kind of mer-chandise of painting they hold to be the visible melodies and harmonies – a kind of visible music – meaning as much and narrating as much as the music which is heard in the ears and nothing whatever more . . . When they paint a woman they do not take the slightest interest in her personally, she is merely, for them, a certain beautiful and fortunate arrangement of forms, an impersonal harmony and melody, melody in harmony, seen instead of being heard. It may seem impossible to many readers that men should even arrive at such a state of mind as this and come to live in the innermost sanctuary of artistic abstraction, seeing the outer world as merely a vision of shapes; but there is no exaggeration in the preceding sentences, they are simply true, and true of men now living.
>
> (P. G. Hammerton, *Contemporary French Painting*, 1868, page 37. Quoted after E. H. Gombrich, 'The Vogue of Abstract Art', *Meditations on a Hobby Horse*, 1971, page 147.)

Seen within the context of this critical tradition Kandinsky's ability to 'overlook' qualities of resemblance in paintings, something about which he boasted in his writings, and the difficulty he apparently experienced in recognizing the subject-matter in one of Monet's *Haystacks*, comes to seem less idiosyncratic, or original than we might have supposed.

There is, however, a considerable gap between merely disregarding the presence and significance of objects in a painting, and conceiving of an 'object-less' art. Furthermore, as I have already suggested, these nineteenth-century critical notions about 'abstraction' were not calls for a totally 'abstract' painting in the accepted sense, and we should not consider them as such. So to what extent was the desire to produce 'object-less' paintings a response to those critical interpretations of modern art which placed particular emphasis on technical processes, rather than on subject-matter – in other words, the kind of theories with which we could identify Kan-dinsky's own interpretation of Manet's work (see page 26).

In the early years of the twentieth century the idea of 'abstract' art was aired by several critics. One has the impression that some of them took it upon themselves actively to encourage the production of 'abstract', or what were sometimes called 'pure' works. For instance, in an article entitled 'Du Sujet Moderne' ('On the Sub-ject in Modern Painting') published in a February issue of the journal *Les Soirées de Paris* in 1912, the French critic Guillaume Apollinaire, noted that 'young painters of the extremist schools wish to make pure painting'. In an article in *Le Temps*, published that October he reported: 'We are evolving towards an entirely new abstract art . . . an art of pure painting'.

The English critic, Roger Fry, was more forthright. In the preface to the catalogue of the Second Post-Impressionist Exhibition held in London in 1912 (see Reader, Text 14) he declared that the 'logical extreme' of contemporary French painting 'would, undoubtedly, be the attempt to give up all resemblance to forms, and to create a purely abstract language – a visual music.' Contemporary aesthetic theory also provided artists with an impetus to create totally 'abstract' works. In his highly influential book, *Art*, published in 1914, Fry's friend, Clive Bell, claimed that all works of art share one particular quality. This he called 'significant form' (see the Reader, Text II). The notion of 'significant form' not only implied that 'the representation of nature was entirely irrelevant to art', it confirmed the idea that a picture might be completely non-representational.

To summarize – even before the beginning of the twentieth century there existed a body of art theory characterized by certain notions: the idea that painting could be autonomous; that elements like colours and forms could have a particular and independent significance; that art could somehow be analogous to music, and that the presence of objects within painting could be disregarded. By the beginning of the twentieth century, critics not only envisaged the possibility of 'abstract' painting, but thought it inevitable that artists would produce such an art.

The myth of Kandinsky's early excursion into abstract art

Much of Kandinsky's reputation rests on the assumption that he was 'the first abstract painter'. Until recently many writers have maintained that Kandinsky produced totally 'abstract' paintings before 1913. For example, in her book *Abstract Art*, 1970, Dora Vallier insists that: 'In 1910 Kandinsky painted his first abstract picture'. 'It was', she claims, 'the event of his life'. I want to investigate Kandinsky's claim to priority, and why, and how, the artist was accorded such an important position in histories of art, and in so doing consider whether questions like 'Who was the first "abstract" artist?' are even worth asking.

As we saw in Part 2, Kandinsky in fact retained vestiges of representational forms in his work of this period. Not one of his pre-First World War statements refers to the existence of an 'abstract' work. Quite the contrary. In 1912 he stated that no artist at the present could restrict his means of expression to the exclusive use of 'pure, abstract forms'. In 'Reminiscences', published the following year, he expressed his theoretical conviction that there could be a kind of painting without objects, but was unclear about how this could be achieved:

> A terrifying abyss of all kinds of questions, a wealth of responsibilities stretched before me. And most important of all: What is to replace the missing object? The danger of ornament revealed itself clearly to me; the dead semblance of stylized forms I found merely repugnant.
>
> (Kandinsky, 'Reminiscences', *Kandinsky. Complete Writings on Art*, page 370.)

He was, however, certain that there would be an 'abstract' art in the future, and proposed that in later years 'pure art will be formed, an art that today hovers before our eyes with indescribable allure, in dreams that slip between our fingers'.

Interestingly, none of Kandinsky's contemporaries referred to him as having painted a totally 'abstract' or 'object-less' picture before the First World War. The most common cause of criticism was Kandinsky's use of colour. In 1910 the German critic, G. J. Wolf ignored the subject-matter of Kandinsky's *Composition 2* (**Pl.VII.48**), and described the painting as an 'involuntary conglomeration of colours'. Another critic, Kurt Küchler, writing in the *Hamburger Fremdenblatt* in 1913, was incensed by what he called Kandinsky's 'madness of colour and form'. He described his paintings as 'Idiotismus' (literally, Idiotism) and 'pseudo-Kunst' (pseudo-art). Apollinaire, writing in 1912, thought Kandinsky's paintings worthy of comment because they showed the influence of Matisse: '. . . Kandinsky carries Matisse's theory of obeying one's instinct to an extreme, the only thing he obeys is chance'. One critic, Curt Glaser, writing in *Die Kunst* in 1912, did associate Kandinsky's painting with the idea of 'absolute' or 'non-objective' art: 'Absolute painting . . . can only be the most abstract, so to speak, the ultimate in art. Kandinsky has demonstrated the possibility of such an art . . . theoretically and practically.' Unfortunately, he did not cite any examples of what he considered to be Kandinsky's 'absolute' paintings.

One might have thought Kandinsky's primacy as an 'abstract' artist would have been mentioned in *Für Kandinsky*, the 3,000-word-long defence of the artist which Herwath Walden published in *Der Stürm* in 1913 after Küchler's attack on him. But this amounts to little more than a collection of meaningless platitudes.

Among the most relevant statements written on Kandinsky's behalf were two by regular contributors to *Der Stürm*, Rudolf Leonhard and Wilhelm Hausenstein. Leonhard insisted that Kandinsky's paintings did contain images. Hausenstein argued that Kandinsky's work was without 'physical motifs'. He did not regard the artist's work as 'abstract', since in his opinion Kandinsky 'translated' emotional feelings into colour equivalents, which were thus representational. This is an important point which will be discussed more fully later.

So how, when, where and why did the myth about Kandinsky having painted a totally 'abstract' painting before 1914 originate? All the evidence points to Kandinsky himself. In 1919, in an autobiographical statement 'Self-Characterization', published in the German journal, *Das Kunstblatt*, Kandinsky claimed to have painted his first 'abstract' painting in 1911 and his first 'object-less' works (etchings) in 1912. Unfortunately, we do not know which works he was referring to, or what he meant by the terms 'abstract' and 'object-less'. His understanding of 'object-less' does not necessarily coincide with our understanding of 'non-objective' (page 6). For example, in 1911 he had used the Russian word *bezpredmetnyi* (literally, object-less) to describe Manet's paintings (see page 26).

In this context he probably meant 'abstracted', 'not concerned with material objects', 'aimless' or 'indeterminate'. By 1919 when he used the term 'object-less' in his 'Self-Characterization' he did mean 'non-objective'. By then he had returned to Russia and would have encountered many examples of geometric 'abstract' art, Malevich's Suprematist works, for example (discussed in Block VIII). It had perhaps become clear that there was a place in history for whoever could most effectively lay claim to being the first 'abstract' artist. His emphasis on the 'spiritual' element in art had already alienated him from the younger generation of Russian artists whose sympathies, at least at that time, were for proletarian democracy. It may have been that this, coupled with the need to assert his own priority, encouraged Kandinsky to emphasize an earlier date for his own 'abstract' works. This was only the first of several retrospective claims that Kandinsky made. After 1927 he refers to an 'abstract' painting of 1911 repeatedly in both articles and letters written to friends and museum directors. As you will see from reading Appendix B, it was only then that Kandinsky mentioned for the first time, the painting which has become known as the 'First Abstract Watercolour' (**Col.pl.VII.2**) which he claimed he had painted in 1910 (see page 58).

Kandinsky's assertions in 1919 that he had painted 'abstract' and 'object-less' works in the early 1910s were quickly taken up by critics. In 1920 Hugo Zehder, the author of the first authorized biography of the artist, wrote, 'Kandinsky painted *the* first abstract picture in 1911', and described his works as without 'objects' or 'content'. Like other 'historians' of 'abstract art' (see the introduction of this block), Zehder never attempted to establish a chronology of Kandinsky's work, and simply referred to his earlier works in the light of later 'abstractions'. Other writers were also determined to make Kandinsky's works as 'abstract' as early as possible. In 1924, Will Grohmann, whose biography of the artist was published in 1958, observed in an article in the German journal *Der Cicerone* that, although one might think that there were still objects in the 1911–1913 paintings, 'by careful concentration one is able to make these figments of our imagination disappear'.

By the 1930s the myth about Kandinsky's early 'abstract' paintings had acquired the status of accepted fact. In 1937 Hilla Rebay, who advised the American collector Solomon R. Guggenheim about his purchases of 'non-objective' arts, started to exhibit Kandinsky's works under the title 'Non-Objective Art'. In her catalogue to the second showing of the *Solomon R. Guggenheim Collection of Non-Objective Paintings*, 1937 (Reader, Text 23), she described Kandinsky as 'the first painter with such intuitive and spiritual freedom as to eliminate entirely the unnecessary hindrance of . . . earthly objects and intellectual subjects with titles and meanings'. She claimed that he had given up 'the help of earthly inspiration' in 1911. The establishment under her directorship of the Museum of Non-Objective Painting in New York in 1939, with its large collection of Kandinsky's paintings, gave further credence to the idea that he was indeed a 'non-objective' artist. (Please read this article now, Reader, Text 23.)

It was only in 1959 that the status of Kandinsky's so-called 'First Abstract Watercolour' (Col.pl.VII.2), and indeed of his other early 'abstract' paintings was discredited for the first time by the art historian, Kenneth Lindsay in a review of Grohmann's biography of the artist, published in the *Art Bulletin*. By this time Kandinsky's 'Cologne Lecture', in which he described how he 'dissolved' images had been published for the first time, 1957 (see Appendix A, page 57). The same year Münter donated to the Städtische Galerie, Munich the large number of works that Kandinsky had left with her for safe keeping in 1914 when he was forced to leave Germany as an alien. This collection was instrumental in the reappraisal of Kandinsky's work, enabling scholars (Lindsay being one of the first) to study large numbers of sketches and paintings from his Munich period. For the first time it was possible to see the extent to which an iconographical scheme underlay Kandinsky's so-called early 'abstract' paintings. It emerged that the 'First Abstract Watercolour' which had contributed so much to Kandinsky's reputation as the 'first abstract painter' was a misdated 1913 sketch for *Composition 7*, also of 1913, a painting based on themes of the Deluge and the Last Judgement (see Col.pl.VII.2, Pls.VII.22–25, and Hamilton, page 212). In Lindsay's opinion Kandinsky dated the watercolour after his return to Germany in 1926, when he collected some of those works he had left with Münter.

The claims, made by Kandinsky in 1919, to have painted 'abstract' and 'object-less' works before 1914 captured the imagination of art historians as late as 1977. That year Hans K. Roethel and Jean K. Benjamin published a photograph of a lost work by Kandinsky in the *Burlington Magazine*, claiming that it was the 1911 work the artist had referred to (page 45). Unfortunately, like the 'First Abstract Watercolour' this painting appears to have been signed and dated at a later time.

Histories and interpretations of 'abstract' art

As we have seen, many art historians and critics, particularly those writing in the 1930s, stressed Kandinsky's priority as the 'first abstract painter' without any evidence to support their claims. How, one might ask, did they arrive at their interpretations of his work? Although it could be argued that Kandinsky's writings bear little relation to his paintings, his pre-World War One essays were not even available for reference at this time (see Appendix A).

In the introduction I outlined one of the ways in which Kandinsky's work and, 'abstract' art, in general was interpreted in the 1930s. You may like to refresh your memory of this by looking at pages 6–10. In the paragraphs that follow, I want to look at another approach to Kandinsky and, by extension, to 'abstract' art in general. From what you have read in your set books, particularly Chipp (pages 126 ff) and Hamilton (pages 157, 205 ff), and Block IV, Part 3, you will probably have noticed that Kandinsky is often classified as an 'Expressionist'. This raises various questions which illuminate the deficiencies and problems involved in just studying him in the context of 'abstract' painting.

1   Why should he be considered an 'Expressionist'?

2   How might such a classification help us understand critical approaches to his work and to 'abstract' art in general? Would placing him in this context help us to understand his work better?

3   What is the relationship between 'abstract' art and 'Expressionism'?

▶ Before continuing you will find it useful to re-read the section on 'Origins of the term: early theories of Expressionism' in Block IV (pages 55 ff), including the Reader Texts, which I will be referring to in the next few paragraphs. ◀

Kandinsky was first referred to as an 'Expressionist' by the German critic, Paul Fechter, whose book *Expressionismus*, the first account of that movement, was published in 1914. As Gill Perry has already pointed out, Fechter identified Kandinsky as the most important representative of what he considered to be a particular tendency of 'Expressionism' – 'intensive expression', which derived its inspiration from 'inner experience'. Like many other critics writing about 'Expressionist' art at about this time (Hausenstein, for instance, see page 45) Fechter did not emphasize the 'abstract' status of Kandinsky's work. He merely described Kandinsky's paintings as 'soul landscapes without the landscape'. There are two possible reasons for this. Firstly, 'abstract' painting as such was not yet identifiable as a characteristic of any particular 'movement'; secondly, as you will have noted from reading Part 3 of Block IV, many critics who wrote about 'Expressionism' tended to think of painting as essentially 'abstracted' from nature anyway – hence the 'opposition' they set up between 'Impressionism' and 'Expressionism'. They often assumed contemporary artists had departed from the faithful representation of nature, because of their desire to capture the 'spiritual' which they considered lay beyond the world of appearance, and because of their 'alienation' from that world. As Gill Perry has already made clear this notion was central to Worringer's book, *Abstraction and Empathy* (see Reader, Text 25).

Many of the characteristics Fechter and Worringer associated with 'Expressionism' were reiterated by the critic and essayist, Hermann Bahr, whose monograph on *Expressionism* was published in 1916.

▶ Please reread the extract from Bahr's book included in the Reader (Text 26) and answer the following questions.

1   Although he did not discuss Kandinsky's work in detail, Bahr found him an interesting artist. Why?

2   How does Bahr inform us about Kandinsky's paintings?

3   What idea of contemporary attitudes towards 'abstraction' can we glean from Bahr's writing? ◀

▷ 1   Bahr is interested in Kandinsky's work because he thinks it 'unprecedented', and because it seems to him to reflect contemporary intellectual concerns: 'this whole pregnant time is one great cry of anguish. Art joins in, into the great darkness she too calls for help, she cries to the spirit' (Reader, page 168).

2   Bahr never refers specifically to any of Kandinsky's paintings. Although elsewhere in his book he claims to be suspicious of what he calls painters' 'programmes', he is evidently attracted by their theories and ideas, rather than by their work. The most informative aspect of Bahr's account is that he locates Kandinsky within a theoretical context.

3   Like other critics of 'Expressionism' already cited, Bahr makes no reference to 'abstract' art, as such. But he does raise several issues which, in retrospect, we have come to identify with 'abstract' art. Bahr distinguished between those artists he called 'Expressionists', from those he called 'Impressionists'. Whereas the Impressionists apparently endeavour 'to rule out every inner response to the outer stimulus' (Reader, page 167), 'Expressionism', on the other hand, is determined by the artists' philosophical rejection of the natural world. Bahr suggests that the 'Expressionist' artist is analogous to 'primitive man': (see Reader pages 166 ff). Bahr's interpretation of 'Expressionism', and by implication 'abstraction' is considerably indebted to Worringer. He had suggested that 'primitive man' was driven by a dread of the 'outside world' (Reader, Text 25), and its 'extended space' to 'instinctively' create a kind of geometrical flat art which 'excluded references to the external world'. Worringer interpreted this kind of artistic creation as one which resulted from 'elemental necessity'. 'Necessity' was a term to which Kandinsky frequently had recourse. Precisely because of his alienation from the 'outward world', Bahr considered that the 'primitive', and by analogy the 'Expressionist', apparently created essentially autonomous works. ◁

After the First World War when the tendency among artists to produce 'abstract' art became more generally discernible, critics concerned with 'Expressionist' art often referred to 'abstraction' as a manifestation of 'Expressionism' – Oswald Herzog, for example. In an article entitled *Der abstrakte Expressionismus* (*Abstract Expressionism*) published in the journal, *Der Stürm* in 1919, he argued that 'abstract' art was 'Expressionism . . . perfected'. As you read through the following extract from his article you'll see that he attributes the same characteristics to 'abstraction' as previous critics had to 'Expressionism'.

> Expressionism is the expression of the spiritual through form . . . In the visual arts the material elements of form are line, surface and light (colour). Abstract Expressionism is Expressionism perfected. It is the purest form of creation. It gives bodily form to spiritual objects. Objects are in themselves whole complexes of expression . . .
>
> For Material Expressionism objects still serve as objects of creation. It abstracts the essence of objects by eliminating everything irrelevant to their purity and greatness . . . Abstract Expressionism is giving form to events – life in itself . . . The artist's intuition takes no account of objects. Life demands only creation. He conjures up forms which are and must be vehicles of his experience. Nothing is random, everything is will, will is art.
>
> (Oswald Herzog, 'Der abstrakte Expressionismus', *Der Stürm*, 1919.)

▶ Please reread the extract from Herzog's article above. What points of comparison do you think there are between his conception of 'Abstract Expressionism' and Kandinsky's of 'abstraction'? You may find it useful to look back to various points raised in the earlier discussion of Kandinsky's theories (pages 31 ff). ◀

▷ The kind of language Herzog used, and the kinds of ideas he expressed are very similar to Kandinsky's. They both focus on concepts like 'spiritual objects'; objects as 'complexes of expression'; 'essences of objects'; artistic 'intuition'; 'conjured-up forms', and so on. Kandinsky's conception of an 'abstract' art evidently bore a close relationship to contemporary theories of 'Expressionism'.

In the preceding paragraphs I have been looking at the relationship between Kandinsky's conception of an 'abstract' art and theories of 'Expressionism'. In order to see why Kandinsky's work has been treated in 'histories' of art the way it has, we also need to consider the extent to which this body of 'Expressionist' theory influenced subsequent interpretations of 'abstract' art. ◁

▶ Please read the following two extracts which are in the Reader. One is from the chapter 'Abstraction and Mysticism' (Text 27) originally published in Sheldon Cheney's 1934 book, *Expressionism in Art*; the other, from Hilla Rebay's essay 'The Beauty of Non-Objectivity', originally published in 1937 (Text 23). As you read the two extracts, try to keep the following questions in mind:

1 What interests do these texts reveal? How do they compare with earlier accounts of 'expressionism', for instance those by Bahr, Fechter, and Herzog.

2 What points of similarity are there between Cheney's account of 'abstract expressionism' and Rebay's interpretation of 'non-objectivity'?

You may find it helpful to look back over the discussion of Expressionism and Modernism in Block IV (pages 58 ff), before answering these questions. ◀

▷ Like earlier writers Cheney suggests that there is an opposition between what he calls 'depiction' (resemblance) and 'expression', and he proposes that in 'Expressionism' the former is held in recession, and the latter increased. He sees 'abstract' art as an extreme development of 'Expressionism'. Unlike his contemporary Barr (see pages 6,7) he considers that even 'formal creation', resulting in a work of 'total abstraction', is inherently meaningful. Like earlier writers, he accounts for that meaning in ambiguous terms, using words like 'spiritual' and 'mystical' to describe it. According to Cheney this kind of art is necessarily produced by an artist who is also a 'mystic' or a 'god'. In this respect his argument is circular, just like Clive Bell's which was discussed in the *Introduction*.

Other interests you might have pointed to are Cheney's notion of there being an 'impulsive urge' towards 'abstraction', its historical 'inevitability'; its appeal to an elite, and its 'messianic' function.

Although Rebay is ostensibly dealing with another art 'movement' – non-objectivity' as opposed to 'expressionism' – her account represents many of the same interests. She claims, for example, that 'non-objective' art has no 'earthly origins' or 'material causes'; that the 'beauty' of 'non-objectivity' is synonymous with its revelation of the 'spiritual' or 'cosmic order'; that such art can only be produced 'intuitively' by the select few. Like Cheney she implies that this kind of art is 'morally good'. ◁

All the passages of critical writings I have asked you to read have been based on similar assumptions, many of which are incompatible. Many critics referred to, for example, have assumed that 'abstract' art has a strictly 'elitist' appeal, and that it expresses the 'unexplainable', yet paradoxically maintain that its function is to educate the 'masses' and ultimately 'induce progress' and 'improve' society. As I pointed out in Part 2, Kandinsky based his work on similar kinds of assumptions, and his work was often interpreted in terms of them (see pages 31 ff and 47 ff). As other block authors have made clear, these kinds of interpretations, as such, cannot be proved 'correct' or 'incorrect'. What we can do, however, is to examine the assumptions upon which they are based – this is what I will be doing in the remainder of this block.

Abstract art, expression and communication

One of the most notorious attacks against modern art and the theories associated with it was made in 1948 by the writer T. H. Robsjohn-Gibbings. In a book called *Mona Lisa's Mustache. A Dissection of Modern Art* he satirized the assumptions upon which contemporary interpretations of modern art and 'abstract' art, in particular, were based.

▶ Please read the short extract from his book reproduced in the *Supplementary Documents*, VII.4. ◀

What Robsjohn-Gibbings found particularly objectionable was the fact that 'abstract' art was presented to the public as being essentially 'esoteric' and incomprehensible to the layman. Above all, he objected to the way that practitioners of modern art were passed off as 'geniuses' and their work as a 'miraculous vision'. As one might expect, Robsjohn-Gibbings attacked Kandinsky particularly viciously:

> Quite frankly, before Kandinsky decided to follow Mme Blavatsky . . . and fling open the door to the 'mysteries', he was not considered any great shakes as a painter. In the large retrospective of his work held in New York in 1914, some of his early canvases were shown, and it was obvious to all but the devout that before the master went in for non-objective painting, he drew and coloured, to put it bluntly, in the manner of quite unmysterious candy-box painters. From the moment, however, that Kandinsky decided to climb onto the esoteric bandwagon of the Theosophists, Cubists and Futurists, things began to look better. Around him . . . gathered the true German believers in the 'mysteries', until finally, thirty years later, the world-wide apotheosis was achieved. In the obituary notices . . . on 19 December, 1944, Kandinsky was hailed as 'pioneer in modern art' . . . and 'pioneer in expressionistic art'.
>
> (T. H. Robsjohn-Gibbings, *Mona Lisa's Mustache*, 1948, page 149)

Subsequent commentators have taken up similar issues, in particular, the problem of the comprehensibility of 'abstract' art. As Robsjohn-Gibbings put it, how are we supposed to know what we are looking at when we look at an 'abstract' painting, and how can we understand what the artist wanted us to feel when we look at his picture?

▶ As you will remember from Part 2, Kandinsky believed that colours not only had their own 'significance', but that they could also exert a particular psychological effect on an observer. Before going on to the next few paragraphs, you may find it useful to re-read the chapter 'The Effect of Colour' from his book *On the Spiritual in Art* (Chipp pages 152–5), and look over your own notes. ◀

In the introduction we saw that various critics writing in the first three decades of the twentieth century maintained that the formal elements in Kandinsky's paintings operated as though they constituted a kind of 'language of the emotions', even though they remained ambivalent as to exactly what it was that was being expressed.

Some more recent commentators, including Ernst Gombrich, are less convinced by the possibility of an 'abstract' visual language. In an essay called 'Expression and Communication' Gombrich specifically tackles the question of communication in the 'non-representational' arts.

▶ Please read Gombrich's essay reprinted in the Reader (Text 28). As you read it, please keep the following question in mind: What disadvantages does Gombrich discern in Kandinsky's belief in the possibility of communicating through 'non-objective' visual langauge? ◀

▷ Gombrich suggests there are two theories according to which elements like forms and colours might be used as vehicles of communication. One theory is what he calls a theory of 'natural response', according to which forms and colours apparently stimulate specific emotions: red, for example, producing an 'effect' of 'warmth and cheerfulness, blue of cold and sadness'. Gombrich thinks this theory constitutes 'the core of the expressionist argument'. However, he considers it to be a very crude theory of communication. It is highly subjective and leads one to suspect that it is only the artist who might understand his or her own paintings. According to a second theory, which Gombrich finds more convincing, forms and tones might communicate like the elements of a conventional language. A 'recipient's' understanding of a work of art, according to this theory, presupposes a knowledge of contemporary painting conventions, and an ability to reconstruct historically the circumstances in which the work was produced.

By way of demonstrating the inadequacy of the 'resonance' theory, particularly as upheld by 'expressionist' painters, Gombrich focuses on the example of Kandinsky. He argues that Ettlinger's account of the sources upon which the artist based his 'abstract' visual language, is too ambiguous to help us understand Kandinsky's paintings. If we are to understand them, we have to look very closely at the kinds of conventions within which Kandinsky worked. He suggests looking at Klee's work, in the same way we looked to the *World of Art* artists, or to Jawlensky in order to understand Kandinsky's earlier paintings. ◁

Conclusion

Gombrich's arguments are interesting for various reasons. For one thing, he points to the inadequacies of certain ideas expressed in Kandinsky's theoretical writings, particularly their inability to help us understand his paintings. He also suggests how invalid many of the interpretations of Kandinsky's work, based on these ideas, are. The truth of this observation is particularly striking if we consider the nature of those writings that were available, particularly during the 1930s (see Appendix A).

One problem affecting the 'histories' and 'interpretations' of Kandinsky's work, and 'abstract' art, in general, has been that his theories are often taken at face value. This may be because many of Kandinsky's ideas were drawn from that body of theory we now identify as the developing Modernism, and later influenced it in turn. Subsequent interpretations of his work were ultimately indebted, often indirectly, to particular ideas expressed in his writings. Certain passages in those writings (although, as we have seen, not all), suggest he believed 'abstract' or 'object-less' art to be a logical extreme of the evolving modern art (see page 44, for example).

Both Kandinsky's own 'abstract' works, and those of other painters, have been interpreted according to such theoretical notions. The paintings' contents are rarely considered, and elements of 'resemblance', which are necessarily of considerable importance to an understanding of the works themselves, ignored. Both Schapiro (*Supplementary Documents* VII.5) and Gombrich propose that 'abstract' art should be approached from a very different point of view: that it deserves the same kind of questioning and scrutiny that allegedly 'less impoverished' paintings (see page 7), in other words those with a higher degree of 'resemblance', receive.

Kandinsky has provided us with a very useful case study, particularly within the context of this course. According to Modernist 'histories' he is one of the most important artists in the development of modern art. But interpreting Kandinsky's work specifically in relation to the Modernist tradition, and in terms of those ideas we identify as characterizing that body of theory, is misleading. His theories were, as we have seen, often inconsistent. They reveal doubts about the validity of particular assumptions usually associated with his writings. This is something never discussed in the 'histories' of 'abstract' art, particularly those written by Modernist critics. Among the questions Kandinsky had problems coming to terms with, for example, were: 'Do intuition and logic have equal status in the production of a work of art?'; 'What should replace the missing object?' And so on. Most important, Kandinsky even doubted, at a certain period, if 'abstract' art was a viable possibility. Certainly none of the works considered in the context of this block conform to Modernist expectations of an 'abstract', autonomous, expressive, formalized kind of art. Quite the contrary, they show us that iconographical or representational schemes were very important to the artist, and that his subject-matter and his manner of painting were grounded within recognizable conventions and practices, usually associated with the kind of art in which there was a high degree of 'resemblance'.

By looking at Kandinsky in relation to the intellectual, social and artistic context within which he worked, I have tried to present a sceptical view of certain assumptions about the artist, and of interpretations of his art, and to suggest how his role within 'histories' of modern art might be reassessed.

References and further reading

Those works marked with an asterisk are recommended for further reading.

Barr, Alfred H. Jnr., *Cubism and Abstract Art*, The Museum of Modern Art, New York, 1936; 1964: 1974.

Bowlt, John, *The Silver Age, Russian Art of the Early 20th Century and the World of Art Group*, Oriental Research Partners, Newtonville, Mass. 1979.

Cheney, Sheldon, *Expressionism in Art*, Tudor Publishing Company, New York, 1962. (First published 1934.)

Eddy, Arthur Jerome, *Cubists and Post Impressionism*, A. C. McClurg and Co., Chicago, 1914 (London, 1915).

Eichner, Johannes, *Kandinsky und Gabriele Münter, von Ursprungen moderner Kunst*, F. Bruckmann, Munich, 1957.

Ettlinger, L. D., *Kandinsky's 'At Rest'*, Oxford University Press, 1961.

Gollek, Rosel, *Der Blaue Reiter im Lenbachhaus München, Katalog der Sammlung in der Städtischen Galerie*, Prestel Verlag, Munich, 1974.

Gombrich, E. H., 'Expression and Communication', and 'The Vogue of Abstract Art', in *Meditations on a Hobby Horse and Other Essays on the Theory of Art*, Phaidon Press, 1971. (See also Reader, Text 28.)

Gordon, Donald A., 'Experimental Psychology and Modern Painting', *Journal of Aesthetics and Art Criticism*, Vol. 9, Part 3, March 1951, pages 227–243.

Gordon, Donald E. *Modern Art Exhibitions 1900–1916. Selected Catalogues and Documentation*, 2 vols, Prestel Verlag, Munich, 1974.

Gray, Camilla, *The Great Experiment: Russian Art 1863–1922*, reprinted as *The Russian Experiment in Art 1863–1922*, Thames and Hudson, 1962.

*Grohmann, Will, *Wassily Kandinsky: Life and Work*, H. N. Abrams, New York, 1958.

Holborn, Hajo, *A History of Modern Germany 1840–1945*, Knopf, 1969.

Hanfstaengl, Erika, *Wassily Kandinsky, Zeichnungen und Aquarelle. Katalog der Sammlung in der Städtischen Galerie im Lenbachhaus, München*, Prestel Verlag, Munich, 1974.

Jelavich, Peter, 'Munich as a Cultural Centre: Politics and the Arts', in the catalogue *Kandinsky in Munich 1896–1914*, Solomon R. Guggenheim Museum, New York, 1982.

*Kandinsky, Wassily, 'Reminiscences', in Robert L. Herbert (ed.), *Modern Artists on Art: Ten Unabridged Essays*, Prentice Hall Inc., New Jersey, 1964.

*Lankheit, Klaus (ed), *The Blaue Reiter Almanac, Edited by Wassily Kandinsky and Franz Marc*, documentary edition, London, Thames and Hudson, 1974.

*Lindsay, Kenneth C. and Peter Vergo (eds). *Kandinsky, Complete Writings on Art*, Faber and Faber, London, and G.K.F. Hall & Co., Boston, 1982.

Rebay, Hilla, 'The Beauty of Non-Objectivity', *Solomon R. Guggenheim Collection of Non-Objective Painting*, second enlarged edition, Philadelphia, 1937. (Reprinted in the Reader, Text 23.)

Ringbom, Sixten, *The Sounding Cosmos: a Study in the Spiritualism of Kandinsky and the Genesis of Abstract Painting*, Abo Akademi, 1970.

Robsjohn-Gibbins, T. H., *Mona Lisa's Mustache. A Dissection of Modern Art*, Adolf Knopf, New York, 1948.

Roditi, Edouard, 'Interview with Gabriele Münter', *Dialogues on Art*, Secker and Warburg, 1960.

Roethel, Hans Konrad, *Kandinsky: Das graphische Werk*, M. Dumont Schauberg, Cologne, 1970.

*Roethel, Hans Konrad, *The Blue Rider*, Praeger Publishers, New York, 1971.

Rudenstine, Angelica Zander, *The Guggenheim Museum Collection: Paintings 1880–1945*, Vol. 1, Solomon R. Guggenheim Museum, New York, 1976.

Schapiro, Meyer, 'The Nature of Abstract Art', *Marxist Quarterly*, 1937; reprinted in *Modern Art 19th and 20th Centuries – selected writings*, New York, 1978, pages 185–211 (see also *Supplementary Documents*, VII.5).

Schopenhauer, Arthur, *The World as Will and Representation* translated by E. J. Payne, Vol. 1, Dover Publications, New York, 1966.

Solomon R. Guggenheim Museum, The, *Kandinsky in Munich 1896–1914*, New York, 1982.

Solomon R. Guggenheim Museum, The, *Vasily Kandinsky, Painting on Glass (Hinterglasmalerei) Anniversary Exhibition*, New York, 1966.

Wadleigh, Henry Rawle, *Munich: History, Monuments, and Art*, J. Fischer Unwin, 1910.

*Washton Long, Rose-Carol, *Kandinsky, The Development of an Abstract Style*, Clarendon Press, 1980.

Weiss, Peg, *Kandinsky in Munich. The Formative Jugendstil Years*, Princeton University Press, New Jersey, 1979.

XX^{e}Siècle, *Homage to Wassily Kandinsky*, L. Amiel, New York, 1976; includes Dora Vallier, 'Colour. His Ariadne's Thread', pages 90 ff.

Appendix A Selected writings by Kandinsky: a chronology

Many of Kandinsky's writings referred to in this block have only recently become available in Kenneth C. Lindsay and Peter Vergo (eds) *Kandinsky. Complete Writings on Art*, Faber, 1982. Interpretations of his work should be considered in relation to those writings that were available at the time.

'Critique of Critics', *Novosti dnia*, Moscow, 1901.

'Correspondence from Munich', *Mir Iskusstva*, St Petersburg, 1902.

'Letters from Munich', *Apollon*, St Petersburg, 1909–10.

'Whither the "New" Art?', *Odesskie novosti*, Odessa, 1911.

Über das Geistige in der Kunst insbesondere in der Malerei (On the Spiritual in Art and Painting in Particular), R. Piper & Co., Munich. 1912: first edition published in December 1911, but bore the date 1912; second, enlarged edition, published Spring 1912; third edition, Autumn 1912; fourth and subsequent editions, edited by Max Bill, Bern, 1952 onwards. Extracts from the book were published in *Der Stürm* (Berlin, 1912); *Camera Work* (New York, 1912), and *Blast* (London, 1914).

Translations of *On the Spiritual in Art*

The Art of Spiritual Harmony, by Michael T. H. Sadler, Houghton Mifflin, Boston and Constable & Co., London, 1914: reissued as *Concerning the Spiritual in Art . . .*, Dover Publications, New York, 1977.

Concerning the Spiritual in Art . . . A version of the 1914 Sadler translation 'with considerable re-translation by Francis Golffing, Michael Harrison and Ferdinand Ostertag', Wittenborn, New York, 1947: 1963 (Documents of Modern Art). This translation incorporates the changes Kandinsky proposed making in 1914, but does so without specific footnotes indicating that these were 1914 additions rather than the original 1912 text.

On the Spiritual in Art, translated and edited by Hilla Rebay, Museum of Non-Objective Painting, New York, 1946.

'O dukhovnom v iskusstve', an abbreviated Russian version of *Über das Geistige . . .* was published in the proceedings of the Pan-Russian Congress of Artists, St Petersburg, 1914.

Translation John E. Bowlt and Rose-Carol Washton Long (eds.), *The Life of Vasilli Kandinsky in Russian Art: A Study of 'On the Spiritual in Art'*, Oriental Research Papers, Newtonville, Mass., 1980.

'Kleine Änderungen zum "Geistigen" ' ('Small Changes to "On the Spiritual"') for the proposed 1914 edition, partly published in Kenneth C. Lindsay, 'Genesis and Meaning of the Cover Design for the First *Blaue Reiter* Exhibition Catalogue', *Art Bulletin*, 35, No. 1. (March, 1953), pages 47–52.

Der Blaue Reiter, edited by Kandinsky and Franz Marc, R. Piper & Co., Munich, 1912 (first edition of 1,100 copies); second edition, 1914; Documentary edition, edited by Klaus Lankheit, Munich, 1965.

Translation *The Blaue Reiter Almanac*, Viking Press, New York and Thames & Hudson, London, 1974 (Documents of Twentieth Century Art).

One of Kandinsky's essays in *Der Blaue Reiter* was 'Über das Formfrage'. An extract from it was published in the catalogue, *Le Fauconnier*, Paris, 1921.

The complete essay was reprinted in Kandinsky, *Essays über Kunst und Künstler*, edited by Max Bill, Hatje, Stuttgart, 1955; Benteli, Bern, 1963.

Translation 'On the Problem of Form' by Kenneth C. Lindsay in Herschel B. Chipp, *Theories of Modern Art* University of California Press, Berkeley & Los Angeles, 1969. (Set book)

Klänge, R. Piper & Co., Munich, 1912? (edition of 345 copies). The terms of Kandinsky's contract with Piper forbade any subsequent editions of the whole volume.

Four poems from *Klänge* were illicitly reproduced in the Russian Futurist publication, *A Slap in the Face of Public Taste*, Moscow 1912. Several translations of poems were included in the 1947 New York translation of *On the Spiritual in Art*.

Translation   *Sounds* by Elizabeth Napier, Yale University Press, New Haven and London, 1981.

Kandinsky 1901–1913, Der Stürm, Berlin, 1913. This included Kandinsky's essays 'Composition 4', 'Composition 6', 'Picture with White Edge', and 'Rückblicke'.

Translations of *Rückblicke* '"Retrospects" by Wassily Kandinsky', edited by Hilla Rebay, The Solomon R. Guggenheim Foundation, New York, 1945.

'Reminiscences', in Robert L. Herbert (ed.), *Modern Artists on Art: Ten Unabridged Essays*, Prentice Hall, Inc., New Jersey, 1964.

A considerably altered Russian version of 'Rückblicke', 'Stupeni' ('Steps') was published in *V. V. Kandinsky, Tekst Khudozhnika*, Fine Art Department for the Commissariat of Enlightenment, Moscow, 1918.

Translation   'Text Artista' by Boris Berg, in *In Memory of Wassily Kandinsky*, edited by Hilla Rebay, Museum of Non-Objective Painting, New York, 1945.

Letters to Arthur Jerome Eddy, in A. J. Eddy, *Cubists and Post-Impressionism*, A.C. McClurg & Co., Chicago, 1914; London, 1915.

'Cologne Lecture', manuscript, 1914; published for the first time in Johannes Eichner, *Kandinsky und Gabriele Münter, von Ursprungen Moderner Kunst*, Bruckmann, Munich, 1957.

'Self-characterization', *Das Kunstblatt*, Potsdam, 1919; republished with minor changes in *Junge Kunst*, Leipzig, 1924.

'Interview with Karl Nierendorf,' 1937; first published as 'Interview: Nierendorf–Kandinsky' in M. Bill (ed.) *Kandinsky: Essays über Kunst und Künstler*, Hatje, Stuttgart, 1955; Benteli, Bern, 1963.

Appendix B   Statements by Kandinsky concerning the production of a 'non-objective' or 'abstract' art.

1912

1   Today, the artist cannot manage exclusively with purely abstract forms. These forms are too imprecise for him. To limit oneself exclusively to the imprecise is to deprive oneself of possibilities, to exclude the purely human and thus impoverish one's means of expression.

(Kandinsky, *On the Spiritual in Art*, 2nd edition, 1912. *Kandinsky, Complete Writings on Art*, page 166)

2   If, even today, we were to begin to dissolve completely the tie that binds us to nature, to direct our energies toward forcible emancipation and content ourselves exclusively with the combination of pure colour and independent form, we would create works having the appearance of geometrical ornament, which would – to put it crudely – be like a tie or a carpet. Beauty of colour and form . . . is not a sufficient aim of art.

(Kandinsky, *On the Spiritual in Art*, 1912. *Kandinsky. Complete Writings on Art*, page 197)

3   In 1914 Kandinsky proposed altering the above paragraph to read:
Today, only a few artists can manage with purely abstract forms. These forms are *often* too imprecise for the artist. *It seems to him* to limit oneself exclusively to the imprecise is to deprive oneself of possibilities, to exclude the purely human and thus impoverish one's means of expression. *At the same time, however, abstract form is, even today, already being experienced as something purely precise and employed as the sole material in pictorial works. External 'impoverishment' is transformed into inner enrichment.*

(Kandinsky 'Small Changes to *On the Spiritual*' for the proposed 1914 edition, unpublished manuscript, *Kandinsky. Complete Writings on Art*, page 877).

1913

4   For me, the province of art and the province of nature . . . became more and more widely separated, until I was able to experience both as completely independent realms. This occurred to the full extent only this year.

(Kandinsky, 'Reminiscences', *Kandinsky. Complete Writings On Art*, page 373).

1914

5   In his 'Cologne Lecture' Kandinsky described how in about 1910:

Objects did not want to, and were not to, disappear altogether from my pictures . . . I was obliged to wait patiently for the hour that would lead my hand to create abstract form . . .

I did not want to banish objects completely. I have in many places spoken at length about the fact that objects, in themselves, have a particular spiritual sound, which can and does serve as the material for all realms of art. And I was still too strongly bound up with the wish to seek purely pictorial forms having *this* spiritual sound. Thus, I dissolved objects to a greater or lesser extent within the same picture, so that they might not all be recognized at once and so that these emotional overtones might be experienced gradually by the spectator, one after another. Here and there, purely abstract forms entered of their own accord, which therefore had to produce a purely pictorial effect without the above mentioned coloration. In other words, I myself was not sufficiently mature to experience purely abstract form without bridging the gap by means of objects. If I had possessed this ability, I would already have created pure, absolute pictures at that time.

(Kandinsky, 'Cologne Lecture', *Kandinsky. Complete Writings On Art*, page 396)

According to the same lecture, it was in 1911 that the artist began to consider what he referred to as 'undreamed-of possibilities':

I felt, with an exactitude I have never yet experienced, that the principal tone, the innate, inner, character of a colour can be redefined *ad infinitum* by its different uses . . . the inner, thousandfold, unlimited values of one and the same quality, the possibility of obtaining and applying infinite series in combination with one single quality, tore open before me the gates of the realm of absolute art.

A spiritual-logical consequence of this experience was the impulse to make the external element of form even more concise, . . . at this point I am speaking not about my own pictures, but about a kind of art that has never yet been personified and in its abstract being still waits for incarnation.

. . . I calmly chose the Resurrection as the theme of *Composition 5* and the Deluge for the sixth . . .

. . . The pictures painted since then have neither any theme as their point of departure, nor any forms of corporeal origin. These occurred without force, quite naturally, and of their own accord. In these latter years, forms that have arisen of their own accord right from the beginning have gained an ever-increasing foothold, and I immersed myself more and more in the manifold value of abstract elements. In this way, abstract forms gained the upper hand and softly but surely crowded out these forms that are of representational origin.

(Kandinsky, 'Cologne Lecture', *Kandinsky. Complete Writings On Art*, pages 398–99)

1919

6   *Kandinsky, Wassily* – painter, printmaker, and author – the first painter to base painting upon purely pictorial means of expression and abandon objects in his pictures . . . [After working at the Ažbè school and under Stuck] He soon began to take part in exhibitions and was condemned by the majority of the critics for his 'exaggerated drawing and messy, strident colours.' . . . He progressed with logical, precise steps on the path that led to pure painting, and gradually removed

objects from his pictures. During the years 1908–1911 he stood almost alone, surrounded by scorn and hatred. Colleagues, the press, and the public labelled him as a charlatan, trickster, or madman. Many wanted to lock him up to prevent his capacity for destruction from causing any further damage . . . In 1911 he painted his first abstract picture, and in 1912 made *inter alia* a series of non-objective etchings.

(Kandinsky, 'Self-Characterization', *Das Kunstblatt*, Potsdam, 1919, *Kandinsky. Complete Writings On Art*, page 431)

1936

7   In a letter of December 16, 1936, written to Hilla Rebay, Kandinsky discussed the categorization of his paintings as 'abstract' or 'non-objective' in relation to the definitions she had proposed in the catalogue to the exhibition of the *Solomon R. Guggenheim Collection of Non-Objective Paintings* that year. (See her essay, 'The Beauty of Non-Objectivity', from the second enlarged catalogue of the *Solomon R. Guggenheim Collection,* reproduced in the Reader, Text 23.)

> As you tell me yourself, you make a firm distinction between 'abstract' and 'non-objective'. The difference, if I understand you correctly, is that 'abstract' means an abstraction from the object, while 'non-objectivity' describes an art which requires no object and therefore uses none. My first 'abstract' painting is in Moscow, and you could certainly call that 'non-objective' since its origin had nothing whatever to do with an object. Since I was unable to continue along that road immediately and without interruption (I was all alone at that time and had no precedents to follow), I returned to the object during the course of the following years. That is, in some of those paintings, traces of an object are visible here and there. However, by 1913 such incidents were rare. The [1913] paintings in the Guggenheim collection such as 'Light Picture' and 'Black Lines' [See Hamilton, page 211] are totally 'non-objective'. So is the large *Composition* 7, 1913. [See **Pls. VII.22–25** and Hamilton, page 212.]

> (Kandinsky, letter to Hilla Rebay, dated December 16, 1936, preserved in the Hilla von Rebay Foundation Archive; quoted after Rudenstine, *Guggenheim Collection*, page 275.)

1937

8   In 1937 Kandinsky granted an interview to the New York dealer, Karl Nierendorf. The interview was not published until 1955, when it was included in Max Bill (ed.), *Kandinsky, Essays über Kunst und Künstler*, Bern, 1955.

> *Date of the first abstract picture?*
> 1911, i.e., twenty-six years ago. Abstract watercolour as early as 1910.

> *How did you arrive at the idea of 'abstract' painting?*
> Difficult to say. Even in very early youth I sensed the unparalleled expressive power of color. I envied musicians, who could create art without 'narrating' anything 'realistic'. Color, however, seemed to me just as expressive and powerful as sound. When I was about twenty, I was sent . . . to the province of Vologda . . . There I saw farmhouses completely covered with painting – non-representational – inside. Ornaments, furniture, crockery, everthing painted. I had the impression I was stepping *into* painting that 'narrated' nothing. A few years later, I saw a large Impressionist exhibition in Moscow, some of which aroused a good deal of controversy, because the painters 'treated objects carelessly'. But I had the impression that *painting itself* had here come to the fore, and wondered whether one could not go a long way further in this direction . . . In 1906 I saw for the first time Matisse's early pictures . . . Much encouraged, I asked myself once again the question whether one might not simply reduce or 'distort' objects, but do away

with them altogether. So I went over to abstract painting, by way of 'Expressionism' . . .

People often say abstract art no longer has any connection with nature. Do you think so too?

No! . . . Abstract painting leaves behind the 'skin' of nature, but not its laws . . .
Art can only be great if it relates directly to cosmic laws and is subordinated to
them. One senses these laws unconsciously if one approaches *nature*, not outward-
ly, but – inwardly. One must be able not merely to see nature, but to *experience* it.
As you see, this has nothing to do with using 'objects'. Absolutely nothing!

('Interview with Karl Nierendorf ' in Lindsay and Vergo (eds.) *Kandinsky. Complete
Writings on Art*, pages 806–7.)

Acknowledgement

Grateful acknowledgement is made to Faber and Faber Ltd. and G. K. Hall & Co.
for permission to reproduce extracts from Kenneth C. Lindsay and Peter Virgo,
Kandinsky: Complete Writings on Art.